Spiritual Development in the State School

A Perspective on Worship and Spirituality in the Education System of England and Wales

How can children 'develop' spiritually and how do their teachers know when 'development' has occurred? This volume aims to trace how traditions of 'school worship' and 'spiritual development' have arisen in the education system of England and Wales, from Victorian times and earlier through to the present day. This involves some consideration of school worship as a potential, if controversial and easily counter-productive, medium for the spiritual development of children.

The subject is examined in various contexts: historical and cultural background; politics and legislation; philosophy and values; curriculum development. The book addresses the issues of spiritual development and school worship, and includes analysis essential for schools and advisory councils in planning new syllabuses and policy statements, offering new insights and a thesis for the way forward.

Terence Copley is Professor of Religious Education in the University of Exeter. He is the author of more than thirty books in the field of religious education, including *Teaching Religion: Fifty Years of Religious Education in England and Wales* (University of Exeter Press, 1997).

SPIRITUAL DEVELOPMENT IN THE STATE SCHOOL

A Perspective on Worship and Spirituality
in the Education System of England and Wales

Terence Copley

UNIVERSITY
of
EXETER
PRESS

First published in 2000 by
University of Exeter Press
Reed Hall, Streatham Drive
Exeter EX4 4QR
UK
www.ex.ac.uk/uep/

British Library Cataloguing in Publication Data
A catalogue record for this book is available
from the British Library.

Paperback ISBN 0 85989 601 3
Hardback ISBN 0 85989 600 5

Typeset in 11/12.5pt Sabon
by XL Publishing Services, Tiverton

Printed in Great Britain by Short Run Press Ltd, Exeter

To Gill, for everything

Contents

Acknowledgements

Jack Priestley was Senior Lecturer in Religious Education at the University of Exeter School of Education when I arrived in September 1988. His generous support helped me rapidly to feel at home. His wise comments, economic and perceptive writing and acute questioning in the field of the spiritual in education were an encouragement to explore it further. Believing that the field is in some sense a treacle sea, I have postponed attempting to chart it until now, concentrating instead on Religious Education. This book is in one sense the result of Jack's unintended stimulus.

In 1995 I interviewed Kenneth Baker, Secretary of State for Education at the time of the Education Reform Act (1988), while researching another book. But the interview record in relation to collective worship has fed into this book as well and for that I am grateful.

In March 1998 I visited Rugby School to read the Arnold papers in the Temple Reading Room. I am most grateful to Rusty MacLean, the archivist, for facilitating this work. Many of the papers had been published by Stanley more than a century ago, but there were some sermons and Arnold's teaching notes among other unpublished items which shed light on the whole corpus and demonstrated that if Stanley's commentary was devoutly hagiographical, his selection of documents was fair.

Finally I record grateful thanks to Gill Copley for help again with the index, a vital but not immediately inspiring task.

Preface

To those outside the complex and sometimes conflicting cultures of the UK, the notion of state schools providing for spiritual development might appear odd, unless the state is a religious one, with a religiously derived constitution. This is not quite the case in the UK, but neither is it the case that the state is totally secular. In England (but not in Wales) there is an established church with the monarch as its head. Churches, alongside other religions, local education authorities, private corporations, charities and individual entrepreneurs, own schools and are stakeholders in education. From 1870 most of the newly created school boards, although secularly constituted, chose to represent religion in their schools. The 1944 and the 1988 Education Acts legislated for universal religious teaching and observance, with safeguards for those wishing to opt out. They did not call for a secular system with safeguards for those wishing to opt in to religious teaching and observance. The evolution of the place of the spiritual in education in England and Wales is a reflection of changing values which can only ultimately be understood in the context of UK history and culture. Attention to or promotion of spirituality, whatever it means in detail, is part of a continuing tradition and intention within UK education.

This book complements *Teaching Religion: Fifty Years of Religious Education in England and Wales* (1997), also published by University of Exeter Press, in which religion as a subject of classroom study was explored. I now aim to trace how traditions of 'spiritual development' have arisen in the educational system of England and Wales. This involves some consideration of school worship as a potential, if controversial and easily counter-productive, medium for the spiritual development of children. The story of the evolution of 'spiritual development' has a theme: that the understanding of spirituality in education arose from a partic-ular Christian value base, best exemplified in the person and extensive posthumous influence of Thomas Arnold of Rugby School. His influence continued in a pervasive and enduring tradition via the Arnold family, the numerous imitators of his headship style, and the development of many schools on the Rugby model. This residual influence only disappeared in the 1960s and 1970s. It is significant that from then on 'spiritual development' in education was largely unhistorical in its self-understanding. Such is still the case. Cultural history and tradition were ignored, adding to the inevitable problems of defining so evasive a field as the spiritual.

It is equally clear that the post-1960s UK values base, although containing residual and frequently underestimated Christian elements, is very different in a society labelled variously plural, secular, post-Christian and post-modern. In such a multifarious culture, spiritual roots will be hard to uncover. One commentator (Erriker, 1998) uses the word 'confusion' advisedly in this context. Crompton (1998) notes similar confusion in United Nations Convention Articles and their treatment of spiritual rights. Wright (1999) talks of declining religion, persistent spirituality. The UK has moved, largely unaware, to a secular model of spiritual development ('a universal anthropological notion', Wright, 1999) and one of the conclusions of this study is that the time has come to examine the spiritualities of religions as potential contributors, reformers or even replacements for this powerful, inadequate and monochrome secular model. This contrasts with the present trend, which treats religions as valuable in so far as they promote 'spiritual development', as if religions are merely steps towards a higher and more enduring universal essence of spirituality.

The 1988 Education Reform Act's controversial requirement for 'broadly Christian' worship in UK schools was influenced by another unexplored tradition, a lingering 'popular Christianity', occasionally articulated by people outside or on the edge of the professional spheres of theology and education, such as C.S. Lewis. It is hard to quantify these extraneous influences on education practice and education legislation and the exercise is necessarily subjective. But to ignore this strand in spiritual development would be to fail to provide an adequate account of how we came to be where we are.

It is not claimed that in seeking to trace spiritual development within a cultural and historical context, this study is in any sense the final word; almost the opposite. As with other explorations into neglected territory, more needs to be done. Limitations of space mean that some aspects of the current and recent discourse about the philosophical aspects of spiritual development, including the nature of personal identity and the feminist contribution, have been neglected. That is not to deny their importance but rather to seek to redress a balance. Similarly, although much of the commentary and many of the issues here can be applied to Scotland and Northern Ireland, their different legal and educational provision make it inaccurate to claim that they have been treated on an equal footing with England and Wales. Space also restricts our main focus to the so-called 'state school', i.e. the county or non-religiously provided school, rather than the religion-based school. Religion-based schools form an important and, with state funding extending to Muslim schools in 1998, growing minority within the UK system. They are not ignored in this text, but they require further treatment in their own right.

Within the UK education system the presence of religious education, collective worship and 'spiritual development' testify, however tokenistic their treatment and precarious their curriculum position has often been, to a continuing conviction that there is more to humankind than the material and utilitarian; that schools are about more than instruction, training, testing and coaching children towards the acquisition of money and jobs. Spiritual development, Religious Education and collective worship as curriculum provision reflect a desire to share with children or help children to undertake for themselves the frequently unsettling but compulsive searching for that verbally elusive Reality that seems to have preoccupied humankind forever.

Terence Copley
School of Education
University of Exeter
November 1999

A footnote on language
It is a characteristic that for much of the period under consideration language was more male-gender oriented than is now the case. Head teachers were often presumed to be 'headmasters'. The child was usually 'he', 'the schoolboy' etc. Quotations reflecting this are allowed to stand verbatim without further comment. The obsequious '*sic*' has been kept to a minimum.

Select Glossary

Education, including religious education, spiritual development and collective worship, has produced a bewildering number of acronyms in the period treated in this text. For the benefit particularly of readers outside the UK education system, a list of the main ones relevant to this study appears below.

Agreed Syllabus—the syllabus pertaining to RE and binding on all county and voluntary controlled schools, part of the 1944 and 1988 legislation affecting RE. It takes its curious name from the requirement that it be agreed locally at a conference consisting of different panels which each have one collective vote in the process.

CCW—the Curriculum Council for Wales, sharing NCC functions and extended to include assessment, later re-named CAAW, Curriculum and Assessment Authority for Wales.

Church schools—in the UK schools owned or part-maintained by churches, mainly Roman Catholic and Anglican, but with a sprinkling of Methodist, Quaker and other denomination schools. Some church schools are entirely independent (i.e. fee-paying). Most are within the maintained sector as voluntary aided or voluntary controlled schools, where the LEA (or the DfEE after 1988 in the case of grant-maintained schools) meets most of the costs.

DES, DfE, DfEE—Department of Education and Science, Department for Education, Department for Education and Employment. Along with Board of Education these are the changing titles from 1944, with some reflection of changing role, of the government department responsible for implementing education policy.

ERA—the Education Reform Act (1988), which for the first time since 1944 legally redefined RE and its position in the curriculum.

GCSE—General Certificate of Secondary Education. This is the external examination system which merged and replaced the old Ordinary ('O') Levels and Certificate of Secondary Education (CSE). These had in turn replaced School Certificate. The GCSE pass grade range ran from A to G, with only U (Unclassified) below it. Fairly rapidly employers and universities began to recognise only the 'higher grade' passes, A to C, which were held to be equivalent to the old 'O' Level.

Grant-maintained schools—schools that after the 1988 Education Reform Act opted by majority parental ballot to leave LEA control and move towards central funding from the DfEE. Becoming grant-maintained, also known as 'opting out', is a one-way move. But the election of a Labour government (1997) led to the start of a process to return grant-maintained schools to some LEA influence.

HMI—Her Majesty's Inspector(ate), i.e. of schools, a member of the pre-privatised Civil Service operation based at the DES, which included a senior inspector for RE. After privatisation HMI numbers were considerably reduced.

KS—Key Stage(s) in the national curriculum. Age 5 children are designated Reception (R); KS1 is age 6 and 7 (Year 1 and Year 2); KS2 is ages 8 to 11 (Years 3, 4, 5, 6—formerly the junior school years); KS3 is ages 12 to 14 (Years 7, 8 and 9); KS4 is ages 15 and 16 (Years 10 and 11). Age 17 is Year 12 and age 18 is Year 13 (the former Upper Sixth Form). Together Years 12 and 13 have been unofficially called Key Stage 5. 'Age' is taken to be the age of the majority of pupils in the year group at the end of the school year. Although the year naming system is optional, it has become almost universal in schools. In secondary schools the following are equivalents:

1st Year	Year 7
2nd Year	Year 8
3rd Year	Year 9
4th Year	Year 10
5th Year	Year 11
Lower Sixth	Year 12
Upper Sixth	Year 13

LEA—Local Education Authority, the area body controlling education (except for independent schools, direct grant schools, voluntary aided schools and after 1988 grant-maintained schools), and itself responsible to its county council or metropolitan borough council.

NCC—National Curriculum Council, York-based, formed to keep all aspects of the curriculum for maintained schools under review, advising Secretaries of State, carrying out research and development work and disseminating information relating to the curriculum. Replaced by SCAA, London-based, and later by QCA, also London-based.

Ofsted—Office for Standards in Education, the privatised education inspectorate after 1988, which was later given the brief to inspect teacher training as well as schools and, later still, LEAs.

PoS—Programmes of Study: the matters, skills and processes which must be taught to pupils in each key stage of the National Curriculum to meet the objectives set out in the attainment targets.

PSE—sometimes known as SPE, or PSME, Personal and Social Education (the added M is Moral), known earlier as moral education. The latest acronym is PSHE, the H being health. Usually non-religious programmes in schools taken by form tutors or non-specialists, which deal with aspects of ethical and personal values. Part of the schooling of all British children. Also important by virtue of what it does not deal with, namely religion as a factor in human motivation and experience.

Public schools—or independent schools, in the UK a term to describe privately owned, fee-paying schools and not as in the US state-funded schools.

QCA—the Qualifications and Curriculum Authority, the London-based quango responsible for curriculum by 1998. It employs a specialist RE officer.

RE—Religious Education, in Victorian times was held to comprise teaching religion in the classroom, 'religious observance' (worship) and what is now implied by 'spiritual development'; after the 1944 Education Act, RE was held to comprise teaching religion in the classroom (Religious Instruction) and school worship. In the 1988 Education Reform Act RE was the name given to the classroom subject only, which thereby emphasised its identity as educational, rather than instructional.

RI—Religious Instruction, the name confirmed for religion as a classroom subject in the 1944 Act.

RS—Religious Studies, the name usually given to RE in external examination studies in secondary schools from the 1970s.

SACRE—Standing Advisory Council on RE, set up in every LEA after the 1988 Act with three (Wales) and four (England) committees to be responsible for advice on RE and worship and for producing and updating the agreed syllabus. An extra committee is added in LEAs where grant-maintained schools reach a specified level.

SCAA—School Curriculum and Assessment Authority, established in London in 1992 to ensure quality in the curriculum and to oversee assessment arrangements, replaced by QCA.

Section 13 inspectors—(from 1996 Section 23 inspectors), inspectors appointed to examine RE, collective worship and spiritual development in voluntary aided schools and the last two in voluntary controlled schools.

'SMSC'—the Spiritual, Moral, Social and Cultural Development of children, a responsibility laid on schools in differing phraseology since 1944 and subject since 1988 to inspection of provision, not outcome.

State schools—strictly an incorrect term but widely used in the UK to denote schools which are not of a religious foundation and are maintained by public funding rather than parental fees. In fact LEAs and dioceses maintain schools in the UK and the only 'state schools' are grant-maintained schools, which are centrally funded and accountable to the DfEE rather than locally. Even so, the powers of ownership and finance that are devolved to their governing bodies mean that even grant-maintained schools are not entirely 'state schools' in a literal sense.

Voluntary-aided schools—one type of church school, in which the church or foundation body appoints two-thirds of the governors and is allowed to require denominational worship and/or RE. Such RE is often in accordance with a diocesan syllabus. It must also be in general accordance with the Trust deed of the school. Such schools may legally advertise to appoint practising members of the foundation religion to serve on the staff.

Voluntary-controlled schools—despite its name, the church or foundation body has only minority control in such a school. They appoint one-third of governors. RE must conform to the LEA agreed syllabus. Teaching is not permitted to be denominational.

Introduction

The Problematic Meanings of Spiritual, Spirituality and Spiritual Development

> Spirituality is often regarded as something warm and cosy, breeding security. There is little support for this in religious tradition. To 'have spirit' may indeed be to possess security, but only in order to face up to and, indeed, to initiate tension. (Priestley, 1982: 5)

Spiritual

Lealman notes that 'spiritual' is a difficult term in that it is 'a vague, imprecise word, one of historical and semantic richness and complexity' (1986: 70). For Webster too it is

> a vague term often used with other equally imprecise words, e.g. development, personality, awareness, maturity and nature. It is also used on [*sic*] contexts which are widely varied and to some degree equivocal, e.g. literary, ecclesiastical, educational, artistic and devotional. It is associated with a medley of often abstract and fustian ideas, attitudes and skills with little coherence or congruence. Never was Wittgenstein's advice to look for the use of words more important than here. (in Tickner and Webster (eds), 1982: 85f).

Spiritual can be the subject of 'edu-babble', defined as 'imprecise and platitudinous rhetoric' (McLaughlin, in Best (ed.), 1996: 17). It is also one of few terms left whereby someone who does not identify with any specific religion can subscribe to that area of human experience previously called religious. In this sense it is easier to conceive of an atheist spirituality rather than an atheist religion, even if Buddhism may lay some claim to the latter.

'Spiritual' also conveniently reflects the current UK ambiguity towards religion. The majority of the UK population do not practise any institutional religion regularly, but neither is the country a nation of self-conscious atheists. Christmas and Easter church services receive a large boost in congregations; many still identify with the Church of England in rites of passage attendance at church: christenings, marriages, funerals and, for a smaller number, confirmation. If the use of the Church of England as a national church is decreasing, it is still real. Christmas continues to engulf the UK culture from July to January and even atheists do not refuse to sing carols, the most intensely theological of Christian hymns. Moreover the Hillsborough football tragedy of 1989 (Davie, 1994: 88–92), the Dunblane school shootings (1996) and especially the death and funeral of Diana, Princess of Wales (1997) led to mass outpourings of grief and mourning rituals that may have been less than institutional religious commitment but were much more than agnosticism or atheism (see p. 82). These were not new in the life of the nation. On 11 November 1920 something similar had been seen at the unveiling of the Whitehall Cenotaph, which stood twelve feet deep in flowers from the public. Its architect, Lutyens, was much in demand to execute similar monuments in other places for a grieving nation. In the case of Diana, many of the messages attached to the flowers and written in books of condolence were addressed to her personally, messages that presupposed she could somehow receive them and was in a state of ongoing existence. The lake-island resting place for a sleeping princess was a powerful symbol of popular emotion with Arthurian undertones. It was a cynosure with all the mystery of Avalon. But interpreting exactly and in detail what these demonstrations of public spirituality indicate is an extremely difficult task.

If the spiritual in British educational discourse has been imbued with imprecision, it is perhaps no more than a reflection of a national sentiment. Coleridge, who was in some ways the genius behind much modern understanding of spirituality, uses the word itself pejoratively: 'The Law, the Prophets and the Gospel teach a series of doctrines so nearly bordering on some recent unpopular tenets that it requires ... interpreters to spiritualise real religion away into a harmless no-meaning' (*Lectures on Politics and Religion*, 1795, 1971 edition: 327). As early as 1795 he detects that spirituality can be devalued into 'a harmless no-meaning'. This warning was forgotten. What spiritual, spirituality and spiritual development have come to mean in common twentieth-century discourse is complex and at times muddled.

Spiritual can also be conceived as the opposite of material or materialistic. It can be seen as less exclusive than religious, which has fallen out of fashion and come to mean religiose or sectarian or pretentious in piety or credal (the taking utterly seriously of certain theistic propositions not in current vogue). 'Religion' may be going the way that 'dogma' and 'propaganda' have earlier gone. Both started out as innocuous words and became pejorative. Many people who are considered to be religious by their peers would find the label insulting. Spiritual has become more acceptable because it is not often used in a religion-specific way: X is less likely to be described as 'a spiritual Jew' than 'a spiritual person'. Einstein's statement that the person who does not know the mysterious and can no longer feel amazement and wonder is 'as good as dead' is cited with approval from a secular humanist anthology (in Wandsworth, 1990: 12) as a spiritual affirmation. 'Spiritual' is therefore being readily applied to non-religious, even atheistic, emotions and ideas. Such common ground across and beyond religions will appeal to educators addressing the 'state school', which may contain pupils from families of all religions represented in the UK and also of non-religious life stances, along with the indifferent or confused on matters of religious adherence and credal conviction. They can all, potentially, qualify as 'spiritual' without loss of their religious, or non-religious, identity. In a climate in which one of the key values of education is to integrate pupils while affirming diversity, such a potentially unifying term will find usage.

Spirituality

Like spiritual, spirituality carries a complex of meanings. Thatcher (1991: 23) identifies it in traditional language as 'the life of prayer and personal discipline' or 'holiness' or 'the knowledge of God'. But it has also come to mean the reservoir of the spiritual in individuals or groups that motivates them, influences their behaviour or points them and those around them to their roots. It is used in this sense by Richardson (1988: 132), as not only self-knowledge but also 'seeing the world as it objectively is, unaffected and uncoloured by one's own projections, hopes, resentments, desires, self-pity ... "enlightenment"'. It tends to be talked of as a resource, positive rather than negative, a factor that helps individuals or groups to cope with life experiences and to find an identity. Lealman (1986: 65) presents spirituality variously as a particular religious discipline; a quality of life, sometimes used in contrast to materialism; an area of thought or writing (as in bookshop shelf labels); and a particular aspect or capacity in human nature. The international conference she reported favoured this latter understanding and defined it further as: a capacity for transcendence; for loss of self; for believing the unbelievable; searching for meaning; practice of silence; awareness of mystery in life; a sort of higher consciousness. However, several of these categories could be applied to Nazism (e.g. loss of self, believing the unbelievable); yet if we can speak of Nazi spirituality, the term has indeed become elastic. But for Lealman, teachers can liberate children's spirituality by legitimising and nurturing all aspects of childhood through activities that enable creating, healing and the transcending of self that can lead to personal growth. By allowing the child to remain within the adult, adults can liberate their own spirituality (Lealman in Best (ed.), 1996: 28). In this context, by implication, spiritual development might mean the liberating of spirituality in oneself and others.

Other recent uses of 'spirituality' have emphasised a non-theistic interiority. Nye and Hay (1996: 145) argue that spirituality can be placed on a spectrum of meaning that runs from 'moral sensitivity' at one end to 'mystical union' with God at the other. For Webster there are three basic elements in the education process: the persons engaged in teaching; the teaching and learning that occurs; and the persons engaged in learning. 'When it is perceived that each of them is grounded in mystery then the spiritual dimension has been approached' (in Francis and Thatcher (eds), 1990: 358). It is a sacramental approach to education. He acknowledges that this is hard to explore, as the balance of education has shifted towards emphasising that which has social utility. Webster's vision for education takes seriously the spiritual:

> It will consider those ideas which today's teachers find embarrassing, like the ineffable or the sublime in education. It will see how what is ineffable inhabits the magnificent and the common, how it is glimpsed continuingly in every fold and

nook of life as well as in what is extraordinary ... sensed in what is beautiful, in acts of goodness, and in the search for truth ... by fostering the realization that there is in life a silent allusion to that which is greater than all life. It was Rabbi Hanokh's view that the real exile of Israel in Egypt was that they had learned to endure it. Without its spiritual dimension, education is in exile. (ibid.: 363)

One problem with this view is that those with the political power to direct education, i.e. UK governments, have rarely interested themselves in what education is all about. They have merely made assumptions and set to work on the basis of those.

Spiritualities and religions

When the word 'spirit' is cut loose from a particular tradition, it gives up a liveliness and passion and turns into a kind of linguistic Lycra, stretching to accommodate any shape or form. It becomes the property of a New Age style Gnosticism, posing as 'the Holistic Option'. It appears that [the London Millennium] Dome theology is going to follow those such as John Hick and Matthew Fox into a humanistic cul-de-sac where all we ever do is talk among ourselves about that which we really cannot talk about. I fear the language of faith will become a kind of spiritual Esperanto which, by trying too hard to belong to everyone, ends up by belonging to no-one. (Gay, 1998)

The traditions of religions seem to be diverse in their spiritualities as well as in their ethics, doctrines and life-styles. No universal essence of spirituality is obvious, other than in a common assumption that there is more to life than the material. Even Otto's attempt to make sense of the many religions he encountered, alongside his personal identity as a Lutheran pastor, finds commonality in holiness understood in a non-moral sense, not in spirituality (see pp. 119ff). His book itself testifies to the divergent spiritualities which he encountered on his global travels. A Sikh may draw on the springs of Sikh spirituality by reading and reflecting on the Guru Granth Sahib, the lives of the gurus, the collective experiences of his or her own family and the senior members of the gurdwara, but such spiritual springs are not as easily accessed or understood by those outside the tradition.

Even Sufism, one expression of one religious tradition, is divided into more different threads: Dhual-Nun in Egypt developed the concept of *marifa*, non-intellectual knowledge, at the same time as Bayazid Bastami, the Iranian ascetic, was trying to reach Allah by removing all human qualities and Muhasibi in Baghdad was emphasising the centrality of Allah summed up in the famous phrase 'Only Allah has the right to say "I"'. These were diverse spiritualities, yet all three men were Muslims, classified as Sufis, and all lived in the ninth century CE. Similarly one can find continuity and discontinuity in Jewish mysticism. Even within religions, therefore, differing spiritualities co-exist and it is hard to generalise about them.

But for Rodger (in Best (ed.), 1996: 46ff.) although there is a burgeoning of interest in spiritualities in recent years, and especially in those from the East, few people have any awareness of western spirituality, nor can they now readily understand it: 'We are like people trying to speak in a foreign language about experiences we have ignored or lost touch with'. Despite this, Rodger refers to tentative taxonomies of the key characteristics of spiritual people, such as by Beck: awareness; breadth of outlook; a holistic outlook; integration; wonder; gratitude; hope; courage; energy; detachment; acceptance; love and gentleness. He then compares Evans's taxonomy: basic trust; humility; self-acceptance; responsibility; self-commitment; friendliness; concern; contemplation (ibid.: 49f.). But Rodger also sees the difficulty of trying to derive general and universal characteristics of spirituality from individual and particular ones.

Spirit in the Bible

In religions, spirituality is best understood as wisdom rather than knowledge, as corporate or individual awareness rather than creed. Even in the Bible there is a complex of meanings. The Hebrew word *ruach* implies breath or wind; the Greek *pneuma* is the same. Spirit is an active force rather than a passive quality. Spirit sometimes carries the implication of dualism: the non-material over against the material; sometimes it presents itself as the real essence of a person, or of God, in action. The spirit of God is 'holy' because God is himself holy: it can only be the 'Holy Spirit' or the 'Spirit of God'. Definitions of a Trinity within the

Godhead came later, although they may be implicitly present in the New Testament record and are occasionally explicitly stated (e.g. Matthew 28.19, John 14.25–9). But in the Bible the spirit is active rather than passive, doing rather than essence, experience rather than contemplation. It has the property of calling to action rather than comforting passivity. It was inspiring; those it inspired acted on it.

Spirituality and the Department for Education and Employment

The Department for Education and Employment (DfEE) has been involved in various pronouncements about spiritual development, collective worship and religious education (e.g. Circulars 3/89 and, notoriously, 1/94). This has led some commentators, notably Hull, to reconstruct a 'theology of the DfEE' (1993) and others to analyse its implicitly secularist approach (Copley, 1997: 129f., 136, 208). The roots of DfEE spirituality are indeed mysterious, but in seeking to understand some of them, note must be taken of the maelstrom sometimes occurring there as a result of the conjunction of junior and senior ministers, civil servants with their own ideas and assumptions, input from the Office for Standards in Education (Ofsted), the Teacher Training Agency and the curriculum authority under its various titles: the National Curriculum Council (NCC), the School Curriculum and Assessment Authority (SCAA) and the Qualifications and Curriculum Authority (QCA) etc. Some of these groupings are rivals. From a research point of view, hard evidence is difficult to acquire and the writer has found it impossible to get detailed answers by letter or interview about how specific policy decisions and content have been arrived at and who has been dominant in the process (for example see Copley, 1997: 177 and footnote 57). In a democracy, such processes should be in the public domain. It is, moreover, perfectly proper to try to reconstruct such influential if hidden processes. Dogma is not the prerogative of religion alone but can pertain in science, medicine, and in this case the politics of education.

Spiritual development

It would be surprising, granted the complex and confusing

meanings accorded to spiritual and spirituality, if the more recent notion of spiritual development were not imbued with an almost inevitable ambiguity and imprecision. The notion of 'development' is not an obvious one in this already unclear context. Hay (1998: 4) also notes a 'natural shyness about the intimacies of the spiritual life' and a widespread anxiety that to testify to experience in this field might lead to one being branded odd, stupid or even mentally disturbed. Froebel took the view that humans are simultaneously spiritual and material beings. Their material self is concerned with the outer world, form and matter, while their spiritual self is concerned with the inner world of mind and spirit. Humans are endowed with 'a vague feeling that this spiritual self has its being and origin in a higher and Supreme Being' (Froebel, 1907: 137). They can sometimes 'see' this more clearly in childhood than adulthood. For Froebel religion itself is not something fixed, but an ever-progressing and ever-present tendency (ibid.: 140). The religious sentiment manifests the unity of all things. Such theistic dualism would not be widely acceptable now and one cannot claim with Froebel that there is an imperative that leads every thoughtful, clear human intellect to a sense of the Unity of all things (McLaughlin in Best (ed.), 1996: 13).

Thatcher (1991: 23) refers to spiritual development as 'an empty and recent concept', which he sees as derivative from a misidentification of spirituality with inwardness (see p. 135), although Thomas Arnold has a version of it, without the vocabulary or the inwardness, as early as 1832 (see p. 27). For Richardson (1988: 132) it is 'one's own, inner spiritual journey' for which one can be taught techniques such as relaxation, visualising, exploring and living with riddles, parables and spiritual folk tales. For Nye and Hay (1996: 145) it is the development of the 'innate spiritual capacity in childhood'. Mott-Thornton (1996: 160) describes spiritual development as the use of the spiritual director or therapist approach. Webster (in Tickner and Webster (eds), 1982: 86f.) notes that the term is 'polysemant' and that attempts to develop the spiritual dimension in young people are 'like a dud photograph—overexposed and under-developed'. For Webster the language used in the domain of the spiritual is of its nature mercurial and elusive, because the notion of the spiritual is ultimately impenetrable. Talk of it is inevitably opaque, but draws attention to what is 'invisible but not illusory' (in Francis and Thatcher (eds), 1990: 357). It will not be easily quantified in a curriculum that heavily quantifies, but this does not excuse us from the attempt to say something intelligible about it.

Kierkegaard's suggestion that the spiritual can only be discerned indirectly appeals to Webster. One possible key to nurture or 'develop' it is religious poetry, which, in Webster's view, consists of the imaginative presentation of experiences of ultimate reality. In evoking the Eternal within and behind all creation, religious poetry unifies the diversity of all things (Webster, 1989: 5). Ungoed-Thomas (in Francis and Thatcher (eds.), 1990: 343) summarises Evelyn Underhill's view of spiritual development: one person jumps a few rungs; a second ascends various steps in parallel; another remains for a long time at one stage, only to proceed with agility and speed through others. Ungoed-Thomas sees development as less a series of sequenced stages and changes but more as converging, interrelated approaches.

Spiritual development calls for clear thinking if it is to be more than synonymous with aesthetic development or personal and social development or a properly emotional response to the richness of life itself or a version of mysticism for schools. Prior to 1944 and after the education Act of that year, religious education was held to embrace religious instruction as a classroom subject and also school worship. By 1988 religious education had changed its legal meaning to become the label for the classroom subject, worship having been customised by teachers and pupils into more user-friendly 'assemblies'; but by 1988 the phrase in increasing use to describe the 'umbrella' previously described as religious education was 'spiritual development'. We are faced with a subject complicated by changing usage and changing meaning of language.

Another, perhaps cynical, alternative avenue of interpretation is to interpret 'spiritual, moral, social and cultural development', a more recent phrase on the education landscape, as a sort of ill-defined holdall, benignly intended to balance National Curriculum prescribed subject content and the vocational emphases especially present in the 14 to 19 curriculum. In such an interpretation it would be fatuous to take any one of the component words— spiritual, moral, social, cultural—and try to define or explore it: they are to be taken collectively to mean that which remains when the subject content of the National Curriculum and religious education have been discharged and the vocational skills addressed. They would have no individual meaning in this

9

interpretation. Such interpretation might well apply to some careless usage of the phrase, but it would be a debasement of language. Each of the words carries its etymology and history separate from its current and possibly temporary educational grouping in what teachers have abbreviated to 'SMSC'. But for Lambourn, spiritual development is simply a 'category mistake', for when 'personal-social' has been distinguished, nothing remains in the category of the spiritual (in Best (ed.), 1996: 150–7). In such an interpretation spiritual development would be a classic case of 'the Emperor's clothes'. The less clearly terms are used and the more secular UK society and the model for spiritual development become, the more appealing Lambourn's analysis will appear. But it will be argued in this study that, confusing as it has become, spiritual development does have both a history and meanings. Moreover, in dispensing with religious vocabulary in an increasingly secular context, one would be then left with either a mind-set that is programmed to delete religions and their claims altogether or with particular emotions—currently included in the spiritual dimension—which we cannot find words to express. Perhaps that is one key to the present dilemma, and the manner and expressions of the public reaction to the death of Diana can be interpreted in this way. Strangled, so to speak, by a secular world-view and vocabulary, the submerged emotions connected with the spiritual suddenly surface in only semi-articulate ways.

Spiritual development seems to have been cut adrift from spirituality as understood by world religions and from what has been for many of them the climax and focus of the encounter with the spirit, worship. The Gospel of John states unequivocally that God is Spirit and that those who worship him must worship him in spirit and in truth (John 4.24). This Judaeo-Christian conviction underpins much of subsequent Christian spirituality, but how does it relate to the secularly inclined 'worship' that takes place in many UK schools or to what British Muslims, Hindus, Sikhs, Baha'i and Buddhists understand spirituality to be? The British Humanist Association is happier with the word 'moral' rather than 'spiritual', and 'assemblies' rather than 'worship', and offers one example of the trend against religious language in the state school.

If school worship emerged in the post-war period as a more obvious and growing problem than spiritual development, capable of provoking pupil, teacher and sometimes parent antagonism, 'spiritual development' within the language of educational discourse was beset with less obvious but equally potent problems. Thinking about it was often shallow and confused. In contrast to the difficulties obviously posed by a confrontational word like worship (everyone assumes they know what worship is and therefore whether they want to be part of it), spiritual development could be a beguiling mist in which one might lose or find the self, but a mist nonetheless. Exploration in the field can be likened to plaiting fog. The whole notion of spiritual development sometimes appears to be a survivor from a liberal, humanist, enlightenment view of humankind which assumed that progress would be upwards and continuous. It appears that pupils are assumed to 'develop', i.e. progress, upwards or 'grow', spiritually. Sometimes upwards is replaced by inwards. But from what and to what end is never clear. If the end of the liberal view of social progress was in the trenches of the Great War, the end of the parallel spiritual view of upward 'development' must be said to have been at Auschwitz. For to espouse seriously any idea of development must surely presuppose an idea of regression. Religions have noted this over millennia by their varying concepts of sin, 'missing the mark' in Hebrew. 'Sin' has been out of fashion in western discourse for some time. Nevertheless the existence of extermination camps, the excesses of totalitarian states and the atrocities of 'ethnic cleansing' throughout the twentieth and earlier centuries provide ample, uncontentious, non-religiously based evidence that humans as individuals and in societies can go backwards in the category of the spiritual; there is no categorical imperative forwards. This is something with which notions of 'spiritual development' in modern education have hardly begun to come to terms. The ancients noticed the inexplicable ruins of ziggurats (tiered towers and temples) around them; perhaps the Hebrew story of the Tower of Babel (Genesis 11.1–9) grew up as an aetiological response, coupled with a wry warning about the tendency to self-deification on the part of humankind. The moderns have forgotten the story. Progress is neither inevitable, nor all upwards.

For Baumann the issue of spiritual development could be seen as one of identity. The modern concept of identity can be traced through Augustine and the Desert Fathers in a metaphor of linear pilgrimage, in which the individual walks towards a destination. Wright also notes this (in Best (ed.), 1996: 139). One might adduce this in very different expressions in Bunyan and Teilhard. The formation of identity has become a task in itself; it has become a problem in the modern period (Baumann, 1996: 20ff.). For Newby, spiritual development is the development of personal identity; the spiritual self is the inner persona, unified and coherent, and 'development' is the process from ill-being to well-being. It is not synonymous with either the religious or the moral life; indeed in a 'post-traditional life' in a democratic and liberal environment, spirituality *per se* must remain agnostic about the nature of humankind's eternal good (Newby in Best (ed.), 1996: 96ff.). Such an approach, if sustained, would cut spirituality adrift from its traditional religious roots entirely and lead in the next generation to a further secularisation of language, although Newby does not wish to close the door on theological realism entirely, despite Cupitt. But in a culture with no 'Master story', only stories, Newby's spiritually developed person has recognisable qualities that provide another taxonomy: to evaluate stories; listen to wisdom; appraise the effects of activities as contributing to the well-being of self and others; reflect on the future; find happiness in that of others; be independent of material wealth; live with uncertainty; practise self-control and possess inner strength. How far these descriptors of spiritually developed people penetrate their 'real' nature and motivation is uncertain. Moses, Jesus, Muhammad and the Buddha may have had these attributes, but somehow extrapolating them into a secular list of qualities does not bring us near to the people. Their real spirituality might arguably lie not in these qualities but beyond them.

The present awkwardness of the word 'worship'

Before the 1988 Education Reform Act the most widely used term by teachers and pupils to refer to school worship was 'assembly'. It was a time-honoured and user-friendly word, which as the 1988 legislators were well aware could in practice embrace a wide variety of activities not remotely describable as worship at all: a visiting puppet theatre; sports results notices; arrangements for fire practice; 'praise and blame' lists of pupils to be seen at the conclusion of the gathering etc. In contrast the word 'worship' seemed restrictive: first it implied a religious premise; worship was seen as an activity engaged in by the religious minority in society. Then it raised another problem: whose model of worship was to be adopted? Inter-faith worship was seen as contentious and undesirable, most often by religious groups themselves, but would a model based on a single faith be any less contentious? By 1997 the Department for Culture, Media and Sport had entered this debate in a pamphlet, *Marking the Millennium in a Multi-Faith Context*, which noted that 'many will not feel comfortable participating in what is experienced as "worship" in another tradition' and commending instead sequential readings from scripture or holy books with shared silent meditation. What is worthy of immediate comment is that this activity is presumed not to be worship. The second point worthy of comment is that the Department for Culture, Media and Sport presumed to comment upon worship at all.

By the 1988 Education Reform Act there were sufficient numbers of humanist, atheist and agnostic people in the teaching profession and in the pupil body to make school worship appear to be an activity that would breach their integrity by apparently attempting to coerce a hypocritical conformity or dividing schools by the large numbers of staff and parents exercising the right to withdraw themselves or their children from the act of worship. Even the use of the phrase '*act* of worship' began to imply a charade. The British Humanist Association, along with many headteachers, was prepared to support 'shared values assemblies', which were intended to build the school community and contribute towards each pupil's sense of personal value, inspiration and purpose by emphasising the shared values of staff and pupils as expressed in the mission statements of many schools. They saw assemblies as a focus for values, to lead children towards a personal commitment to agreed moral values. But they were opposed to any notion of worship as understood by religions being imposed on staff or pupils. Not many people were prepared to enter a debate about how far their assumptions about what 'worship' means were actually justified, nor to see the debate about worship in its context of the whole question of the values underpinning education. Fewer Victorian values had disappeared than many imagined: education was still seen by many, including some newspapers, as an antidote to social disorder (Copley, 1997: 157f.) or a free child-minding service, as witnessed by the frequently antipathetic parental reactions to most of the rare teachers' strikes after 1945.

Over the period we are considering, school worship was at first the assumed partner of Religious Instruction (RI) (as it then was called) and was viewed rather like the practical lesson in science, a partner of the classroom theory. Children were intended to learn their religion in the classroom and practise it in the hall. RI and worship were both assumed to be Christian in character. *Songs of Praise* was a staple diet for school hymnody, selling in various editions from 1925 up to the publication of this book. But as the years advanced, religious educators sought to distance themselves from school worship and to emphasise the separateness and distinction between religious education and worship, such that by the end of the twentieth century school worship had become an orphan in curriculum terms. No curriculum subject 'owned' it; no staff were trained to lead it; no teacher education course provided for it in any depth, if provision were made at all; rarely if ever was a rationale for engaging in it offered to pupils and almost no research was being undertaken into it. Generations of children brought up from the 1960s to question all aspects of their learning found no ready answers as to why they were subjected to worship, except the very unsatisfactory reason of legal compulsion. Unsurprisingly, many teachers and pupils in secondary schools in particular came to view it as an anachronistic and otiose chore. They did not as readily see that this view was conditioned by the extraneous factors listed. Had any curriculum activity been starved of resources, staff training, debate about rationale etc. in the way in which worship had been, it would probably have received an equally sceptical response.

Even the churches, which in earlier generations might have backed school worship strongly, increasingly came to admit the practical difficulties and were more prepared to surrender the 'daily' clause, without addressing the philosophical difficulties that worship of any sort in the state school system poses. In an apparently secular society, the whole question of compulsory worship appeared to be philosophically inconsistent (can one compel others to worship?) and morally dubious (since adult worship is apparently a minority preoccupation, on what grounds should it be enforced on the majority of children?). The legal requirement that such worship should be daily was viewed by many as inimical of quality. Yet for many adults, primary school worship in particular remains a compelling and sometimes pleasurable memory. To some extent the dilemma and the problems associated with spiritual development and worship in state schools are specific to the UK context and historical development of education.

The Humpty Dumpty syndrome

Without being facetious, one can note the Humpty Dumpty syndrome in relation to spiritual development, namely the tendency to ascribe meanings in the face of uncertainty:

> 'When *I* use a word', Humpty Dumpty said in a rather scornful tone, 'it means just what I choose it to mean—neither more nor less.'
>
> 'The question is', said Alice, 'whether you *can* make words mean different things.'
>
> 'The question is', said Humpty Dumpty, 'which is to be master—that's all ... When I make a word do a lot of work ... I always pay it extra.' (Carroll, 1871, 1977 edition: 74f.)

White, writing from a humanist perspective, has already made use of Humpty Dumpty and 'impenetrability' (in Best (ed.), 1996: 30–5).

Humpty Dumpty provides historical coincidence as well as an apt metaphor. Historically, the well-known rhyme appeared in print *c.* 1803. Charles Dodgson (Lewis Carroll) provided the conversation with Alice in 1871 and gave Humpty a donnish identity. Dodson, a Mathematics don himself, had been an unhappy pupil at Rugby for three years during the headship of A.C. Tait, later Archbishop of Canterbury. *Alice* contains some echoes of this, e.g. the Caucus Race is a parody of school games (Cohen, 1995: 139). As a clergyman, Dodgson adopted a broad church position in the tradition of Rugby head Thomas Arnold in contrast to the unbending views of his own clerical father. That the Humpty Dumpty conversation was written by a Rugbeian is coincidence. But it will be claimed in Chapter 1 that in tracing spiritual development in Victorian times and in understanding how we have come to be where we are now, all roads lead to Rugby.

Chapter One

The Context in UK Culture and Society

The early nineteenth-century context

In the early nineteenth century, education in schools and in the two universities was very much dominated by the churches. The Anglican church was the established church in England and Wales. 'Tests' restricted degrees at Cambridge to Anglicans and filtered admission to Oxford. Nonconformists had founded rival dissenting academies and although more liberal in admissions policy and in curriculum than the universities, they remained essentially Christian institutions. University dons were almost always ordained and always Anglicans. Public school heads were also Anglican clergy. Methodist, Quaker and other nonconformist schools were controlled by their respective denominations, by Conference and committee respectively.

The mood behind the elementary school provision system was one of philanthropy, carried over from eighteenth-century attitudes to the poor. It was as providers of education that the churches exercised a degree of social influence and control. The National Society for the Education of the Poor in the Principles of the Established Church had been founded in 1811 to spread elementary education. The nonconformist equivalent was the British and Foreign Schools Society, founded earlier, in 1807. Sunday schools were also provided to teach the three Rs, often in two three-hour sessions on Sunday. In this way it was assumed that the purposes of Sunday schools and purposes of day schools were much the same, one having five days in which to provide the teaching and the other only one. The reduction of Sunday schools to Christian catechetical work was not to come until free universal elementary education was provided by the state, after 1870. But it continued to be assumed into the 1950s that religion in the day school and in the Sunday school were complementary.

Anglicans and nonconformists were rivals in education provision and nonconformists grew frustrated with their legal disability and resented the power and privileges of Anglican establishment. Anglicans would go on to open colleges to train teachers for elementary schools such as St Mark's, Chelsea (1841). Nonconformists would respond by institutions such as Westhill College, Birmingham. But despite their rivalry, both groups shared a common assumption: that education was a natural role for the church to engage in and that education was unquestionably a Christian activity. It was thought inappropriate for the state to concern itself directly with the provision of schools or with the teaching of religion. The first government intervention in education came mutedly, in the form of a grant of £20,000 for school building costs made in 1833 to facilitate the development of elementary education and to be divided between and administered by the two rival societies.

The later nineteenth-century context

By mid-century there was more polarisation. The nonconformist lobby for disestablishment of the Anglican church and for removal of the church rate, which could be levied to support what was seen as the 'state church', was stronger. A Roman Catholic lobby had arisen, eager to provide fully denominational schools for their own children. A 'Voluntaryist' movement arose from 1843 led by Edward Miall, an Independent (Congregational) minister and editor of *The Nonconformist*. It campaigned for schools to be entirely independent of the state. By 1851 Voluntaryists had financed 364 schools and one teacher training college. Anglicans too had become more vigorous in their demands. Archdeacon Denison of Taunton, a champion of the Oxford Movement, argued that religious instruction could never be unsectarian and must be an integral part of all education, and that education therefore lay within the province of the church and not the state.

Alongside the growth of full-time, but not yet universal, elementary education there continued the existence of various part-time alternatives: Sunday schools, 'ragged schools' for children of the poor, and half-time education for factory children. One of the most radical schools of its day, the Manchester Model

Secular School (founded 1854), was secular only in that it was not under denominational control and it did not promote 'dogmatic' teaching. Sponsored by industrialists, at least sixteen of its two dozen promoters were Christians, ten of them Unitarians. The curriculum was utilitarian in every aspect including 'religion'. The school claimed to be 'religious in its tendency' by providing discourses on practical morality intended to foster 'a love of truth, honesty, temperance, cleanliness, punctuality and order; obedience and love of parents, respect for teachers and kindness to each other' (D.K. Jones in McCann (ed.), 1977: 127). Jones argues that the pressure for religious instruction came from middle-class rather than working-class parents. He believes that the latter viewed the religious teaching in schools with indifference and were concerned to secure for their children the best secular education available.

The Christian dominance of schooling was almost complete and almost universally acceptable, or at least unchallenged, except among the small but vocal minority of atheist secularists. Within this context of overwhelming acceptance of the place of Christianity in education, it seemed natural for schools to provide religious instruction, acts of worship and, in schools controlled by credal churches like the Anglican and Roman, catechetical instruction, e.g. confirmation preparation. Where there was pressure to stop the latter, it came mainly from nonconformists who found their children obliged to attend, by virtue of lack of nonconformist school provision in proximity to their home base. At the same time, States within the Union in the USA were facing similar problems of sectarian rivalry and competition for public funding for schools, but were appealing to the different solution of a secularised school system with religious teaching forbidden in the publicly funded school. This meant that nothing comparable to UK RE could develop in the USA, yet, paradoxically, secular state rituals in schools such as flag-saluting ceremonies evolved in parallel to school worship rituals in the UK. That the world's greatest democracy, the USA, could not handle religion in the school context continues to appear incomprehensible to UK onlookers.

By 1853 state financial aid to education in the UK had reached about £250,000. But the Newcastle Commission (1861), a royal commission produced by and for the state, could still oppose the direct state control of schools. It proposed, at the time unsuccessfully, that money for education should be raised from local rates. What was clear was that with the growing population and the education needs of a rapidly industrialising country with growing colonies, the churches simply did not have the resources in plant or finance to meet the situation. But however clear the economic reality was, it was not accepted unopposed. The National Educational League (founded 1869) accepted that a national system would be required, but argued for it being locally rate-financed and locally controlled. The rival National Education Union wanted central funding to preserve and extend denominational schools. Bitter as the arguments became, once again the Christian values underpinning the education process were not the subject of the controversy. So uncontroversial was the Christian value base, that it was rarely stated in explicit terms. The 1870 Education Act's references to the issue are discussed on pp. 57–62.

Thomas Arnold (1795–1842)

While the state was trying to keep out of direct involvement with education and the churches were concerned to raise money and to fight for school territorial expansion, it was left to individuals to develop the vision that would enable education to start to cope with a rapidly changing and newly industrialised world. Thomas Arnold was a Victorian for only five years, but his national influence was to come in late Victorian times and beyond. Like his short-lived contemporaries Ann and Emily Brontë, who survive largely through the filter posthumously created by their sister Charlotte and her friend Elizabeth Gaskell, Arnold's image has been filtered through the medium of two different but highly influential portraits, that of his former pupil Thomas Hughes in the novel *Tom Brown's Schooldays* (1857) and that of another former pupil, Arthur Penryn Stanley, in a hagiography, *The Life and Correspondence of Thomas Arnold* (1844, 1845 edition). Even as early as 1897 Hughes's account was viewed by some as 'a romance' (Fitch, 1897: 104). Hughes himself in the sequel (1861: ix) responds that the only non-fictitious character in the book is Arnold. One commentator reduced Arnold to notable and influential but 'not positively great' as early as 1902 (Saintsbury, 1902: 3). Despite this, for fifty years the Hughes–Stanley portrait set Arnold's image, often inaccurately, until he was lampooned in the iconoclastic essay by Giles Lytton Strachey in *Eminent Victorians* (1918).

The 1885 *Dictionary of National Biography* entry for Arnold argues that there was 'nothing startling' in his reforms, 'nor was there anything recondite in his system' (Stephen (ed.), 1885: 114). But Theodore Walrond, the writer of the article, had the advantage and disadvantage of being a former Rugby pupil, teacher and an unsuccessful candidate for the headship in 1870, which might account for his testiness. More recently another biographer presents Arnold as of no original educational significance and writes that 'the mind of this man, usually considered to be the greatest of headmasters, was really interested fundamentally in the world outside the [Rugby School] Close' (Bamford, 1960: 212). For Bamford, Arnold's distinctiveness lay only in the powers of allowing the sixth form to flog younger boys and in the cultivation of an intense religious attitude among boys (ibid.: 189). Arnold can even be made to appear avaricious. He certainly wrote that 'money tempted me' to stand for Rugby, but he had a rapidly growing family and other dependants and in the same letter added 'I should like to try whether my notions of Christian education are really impracticable' (30 November 1827, in Stanley, 1844, 1845 edition: 86). Shortly after he wrote of his hope to make the school 'an instrument of God's glory, and of the everlasting good of those who come to it' (28 December 1827, ibid.: 86), hardly a half-hearted statement by one whose real interests lay elsewhere, unless one interprets it as a pious cliché.

Caution is therefore required in trying to reconstruct Arnold's values and his real contribution to UK education. Nevertheless, it will be argued that Arnold is one of the most significant figures in the development of the spiritual in English education and that this influence was manifest through various channels: his own writing; the Arnold dynasty; the post-Arnoldian tradition at Rugby, especially in Frederick Temple; the Old Boys who became heads on the Rugby style; and the unquestioned deep impression of his personality on those he encountered. Even Bamford concedes that Arnold was the one headteacher of the period who was a real national presence outside the classroom. He brought 'the zeal of the Crusader into what the world persists in thinking a prosaic profession' (Whitridge, 1928: 214). Attention will be paid to his career and ideas here because in his person Arnold bridged the gap between the worlds of education and theology and because he was the most significant Victorian contributor to the notion of the spiritual development of children, although he used the phrase 'religious education' to mean what is now referred to as spiritual development. Arnold's significance for an understanding of spiritual development has been largely forgotten. By the time Collingwood wrote a chapter on Rugby, Arnold is not even mentioned (Collingwood, 1939, 1970 edition: 7–14), and Collingwood, though a difficult pupil, had been an accomplished classicist at the school.

Arnold outside Rugby

Arnold was no stranger to controversy. His strong support for Catholic emancipation (1828) cost him the Archbishopric of Ireland in 1831. A broad church man in the tradition of S.T. Coleridge, whose own *Confessions of an Enquiring Spirit* had to be published posthumously, he was within a clear minority in the church in his life-time. Arnold was a critical admirer of Coleridge: 'with all his faults old Sam was more of a great man than anyone who has lived within the four seas in my memory' (in Fallows, 1963: 276). He was also a personal friend of Coleridge's nephew, Judge J.T. Coleridge (1790–1876). This was the 'seed time' of the broad church, whose harvest could be described as from 1848 to the present day (Sanders, 1942: 91). The 'broad church' was less a party in the Church of England than a mood or approach that was prepared to accept biblical criticism and to attempt to find a bridge between Christianity and modern thought. By late Victorian times a conservative version of this approach was extremely influential, even dominant, in the church, further enhancing Arnold's posthumous influence. Arnold also clearly saw the failure of the churches to capture the masses and the need to reform the church in order to achieve this, including the creation of smaller dioceses and the adoption of more collegiality in church government. But in his life-time his broad church and Whig sympathies were suspect. He made a two-day journey from the Lakes to Rugby in 1835 to vote for the Radical candidate for Parliament rather than the Tory, although the Tory was a son of one of the Rugby School trustees and the father of a Rugby pupil.

In 1836 Arnold made national controversial news with an anonymous essay in the *Edinburgh Review*, 'The Oxford

Malignants'. The title was not his, but it expressed his sentiments perfectly. It was a passionate broad church attack on the emerging Oxford Movement in the Church of England. They were cast as formalising, Judaising fanatics, 'ever the peculiar disgrace of the Church of England'. His authorship became an open secret, which nearly cost him his job. A vote of censure against him in a meeting of the school's trustees split 4–4, but as their constitution allowed for no casting vote, the matter had to be dropped. In 1838 he appeared in further public dispute, defending a case in Chancery brought because, contrary to the foundation deeds of the school, he was deliberately allowing the Lower School to decline. This discriminated against local boys, who as foundation pupils of the original free grammar school needed places there to have a chance of gaining the coveted education of the Upper School. His attack on the notion of factory workers as 'hands', his criticism of the growing National Debt, his denunciation of Freemasonry, all made him appear to those outside Rugby a vitriolic, even dangerous, influence on youth and his clarion call for church reform clearly lost him a bishopric. Yet he neither entirely fitted the label conservative or radical. Arnold was at times a radical conservative; at others he seemed a conservative radical. He was not a party man.

Famed for his view that the Church of England could be reconstituted to accommodate all branches of Christianity except Unitarian, even to include Roman Catholic, Arnold was opposed to the religious tests that had applied for admission to Oxford and degrees at Cambridge and effectively restricted places to Anglicans. Before Rugby he had been willing to stand for a Chair in History at the new London University; he later accepted a seat on its Senate (1836) with alacrity. He quickly proposed that a study of one of the gospels or epistles of the New Testament in the original Greek should be a compulsory part of the course for every candidate in Arts. He was clear that this was part of the complete and liberal education which an Arts graduate should have and that in a Christian country a liberal education without an element of the Scriptures must necessarily be incomplete. But the other senators saw this as redolent of the tests that they prided themselves on London having abjured, so his proposal was defeated, although an optional study in the field became the precursor of the Associate of King's College (AKC) and other certificates. Arnold resigned over the matter in 1838.

In 1841 the death of the Regius Professor of Modern History at Oxford led to Arnold's appointment. He had behind him a significant publications list, not all modern history, including encyclopaedia articles, three volumes on Thucydides, an unfinished *History of Rome*, and thirteen articles on 'the social condition' published in the *Sheffield Courant*. His intention was to stay on at Rugby and lecture in Oxford on an occasional basis, until such time as he might retire from headship. Despite fears that he would use his Chair as a pulpit from which to denounce Tractarianism, leading to a gladiatorial audience of about four hundred in eager anticipation in his first lecture series, he consciously adopted a manner of forbearance and restraint. He returned to Rugby in the Lent Term of 1842 to news of his daughter Jane's engagement being broken off by the teacher she was due to marry. Arnold collapsed and although he appeared to recover from this, he died a month later.

Arnold at Rugby

Arnold had arrived as head at Rugby School with his family by stage coach in August 1828, his furniture arriving more slowly by the Grand Junction Canal. His faster arrival was perhaps symbolic of what one commentator has described as his 'massive energy, an inexhaustible industry, a galvanatic personality, and a vigorous intellect ... fused in him by the central power of complete moral certitude' (Biswas, 1972: 13). A reluctant and last-minute applicant for the post, he had been appointed head from about fifty candidates without interview on the basis of testimonials, according to custom. Hawkins's testimonial stated that if appointed, Arnold would change the face of education through all the public schools of England. Rugby was a considerable promotion, as the establishment Arnold was running in his house at the time in Laleham did not have ten boys on roll. He was really a private tutor until Rugby.

The 'Rugby rebellions' were still within living memory in the town; these had taken place between 1770 and 1818, on at least two occasions requiring soldiers to quell them, although Arnold's predecessor John Wooll passed on a reasonably ordered school by contemporary standards. Arnold brought to the school 'an image of vehement righteousness' (Murray, 1996: 7). There is more than a hint of this in the firm jaw, the set eyes and the slightly wild hair in the 1839 portrait by Thomas Phillips. Arnold took headship very seriously as a high calling. He had

> a most sincere desire to make it a place of Christian education … to form Christian men, for Christian boys I can scarcely hope to make; I mean that from the natural imperfect state of boyhood, they are not susceptible of Christian principles in their full development … and I suspect that a low standard of morals in many respects must be tolerated amongst them. But I believe that a great deal may be done … [2.3.1828, in Stanley, 1844, 1845 edition: 88]

In a letter to a newly appointed teacher he wrote: 'The qualifications which I deem essential to the due performance of a master's duties here, may in brief, be expressed as the spirit of a Christian and a gentleman' (ibid.: 107). On the occasion of the unpopular expulsion of a number of boys, Arnold stood before the whole school and said: 'It is not necessary that this should be a school of three hundred, or one hundred, or of fifty boys, but it *is* necessary that it should be a school of Christian gentlemen' (ibid.: 117).

Stanley presents Arnold as averse to flogging, except for the offences of lying, drinking and habitual idleness, and then only among the younger boys, but by 1833 he had fallen foul of the *Northampton Herald* for publicly flogging a fourteen-year-old boy called March with eighteen strokes for persistent lying. Even Hughes concedes Arnold's ire was well-known and that there were discernible signals: 'the Doctor's under lip was coming out, and his eye beginning to burn, and his gown getting gathered up more and more tightly in his left hand' (Hughes, 1857, 1994 edition: 142). On the basis of misinformation supplied by March's housemaster, Arnold had examined the boy on a translation passage he was supposed to have prepared from Xenophon. The boy strenuously denied he had been told to prepare this and was flogged for repeatedly lying. Despite a public apology to the boy in front of the entire school, which Arnold volunteered, and a written apology to his parents—and this at a time when flogging was the norm—the press attacked him, not for the use of flogging *per se*, but on the basis that if lying produced this punishment, what must more serious offences incur? But for Arnold there was no more serious offence. He insisted that he would trust what his pupils told him, a radical departure in education, to which they generally responded well. Breach of trust was to him breach of the most basic relationship between teacher and pupil. He expected no less of himself: it would be foolish and inconsistent for a person to live like a heathen and profess to believe as a Christian (*Sermons*, 1832, 1850 edition: 278). Despite the extraordinary and indefensible nature of this particular punishment, he wished to see flogging reduced both in the number of times it was administered and the number of strokes. Arnold was very much opposed to the existing tradition of headship that flogged miscreants for all offences for which they were presumed guilty. Nor did he feel it was an appropriate punishment for older boys. When the matter became public it was he who corrected the statement that March had received fifteen strokes to eighteen in the interests of truth. He was prepared quietly to expel the worst trouble-makers (the bully Flashman was characteristically dispatched without ceremony first thing in the morning after his final offence) and to advise the parents of pupils making no progress to withdraw them, despite the fears of his trustees that numbers in the school would reduce. In fact they rose. 'Till a man learns that the first, second and third duty of the schoolmaster is to get rid of unpromising subjects, a great public school will not be what it might be, and what it ought to be' (ibid.: 127). If this seems harsh in a climate more sensitive to the special needs of children, it must also be set in a context in which 'dull' children were sometimes retained in their schools as a source of income, despite themselves and their peers deriving no benefit from their presence.

Many of the reforms of public school education which were later credited to Arnold—strengthening of the prefectorial system, modernising the curriculum, developing a cult of compulsory, organised games including Rugby football (1823)—were either not original to him, or were wrongly attributed. Arnold was opposed to major curriculum reform. French at Rugby had a very subsidiary role, Science almost none (despite Trevor, 1973: 27), and he was indifferent to compulsory, organised games. Fitch (1897: 37, 50f.) suggests that Arnold put new life into received methods of teaching rather than inventing new ones, bringing to the task commitment and enthusiasm. One of his reforms at Rugby was to replace 'dames', non-teaching women who took in boarders, with housemasters, teachers who took on boarding supervision duties. He became head of School House himself. The pupils' petition to ask him to carry on in this capacity when he proposed to lay it down to concentrate on other duties still survives at Rugby. He abolished the school hounds pack; reduced the extent of fights between boys and regulated the occasions of them; he reduced the poaching and vandalism practised against local farmers and restricted the extent of fagging. He enhanced but also regulated the powers of praepostors (prefects) and 'Tom Brown' could look back as an Oxford undergraduate on his own part 'in the ruling of 300 boys, and a good deal of responsibility' (Hughes, 1861: 39). Arnold significantly raised the status of his teachers by raising their salaries so that they were not obliged to take on local curacies to make ends meet. If these were not all original, they were effective reforms.

What made Arnold original in education was his 'single-minded, fierce determination to turn out Christian gentlemen' (McCrum, 1989), 'his unwearied zeal in creating "moral thoughtfulness" in every boy with whom he came into personal contact' (Hughes, 1857, 1994 edition: 16). But he did not believe that this could be done by extra religion classes or more compulsory Chapel services, but by what would now be called whole-school ethos. He did not distinguish between religious and secular instruction and made it his chief task to Christianise the school, taking on himself the role of chaplain and preaching on most Sundays to the gathered boys in the two services. Although he wished to waive the extra income from the chaplaincy (£60 per annum), the trustees insisted he have it. Arnold used the money to improve the library. Registration after Chapel was abandoned in favour of a seemly silence as pupils left the building, filing past Arnold, who remained in his place watching them. Voluntary communion services, on four occasions per year, were routinely attended by between seventy and a hundred, out of about three hundred pupils.

But Arnold valued the opportunity provided by preaching, and after taking on the chaplaincy he preached on almost every term-time Sunday until his death. No sermons lasted more than twenty minutes (short by contemporary standards) and none was repeated. They were composed between the morning and afternoon services. The neatly written notebooks of them survive. The early themes were the sources of evils in schools and the pure moral law of Christianity. The misconduct of individuals was not mentioned. The tone was of entreaty, to take up arms against evil. Faith was presented as firstly a natural attitude for humankind, e.g. faith in the advice that parents offer; then as 'the feeling of preferring the future and the unseen to the present ... [a feeling which] would raise and improve the mind; then faith in God, the heavenly parent'; then finally in God as known to Christians, 'God as the Father of our Lord Jesus Christ' (*Sermons*, 1832, 1850 edition: 6ff.). The sermon emphasis was on individual integrity and on personal and collective effort. The Sunday evening prayer at the School House included the searching passage: 'Thou knowest, O Lord, and our own consciences each know also, whether while we worshipped Thee in form we worshipped Thee in spirit and in truth' (in Stanley, 1844, 1845 edition: 348). Arnold's contribution to a book of family prayers included an entreaty he personally fulfilled: 'Let us rise early and go late to rest, being ever busy and zealous in doing Thy will' (ibid.: 354). The daily pre-lesson prayer for the sixth form was: 'O Lord, stengthen the faculties of our minds and dispose us to exert them' (in Whitridge, 1928: 111). He awarded prizes for effort as well as achievement, at his own expense.

Arnold made himself personally available to pupils, not just the sixth form, and from 1831 his presence in his study was advertised by a flag outside, a public invitation to call. Pupils availed themselves of this. They were also invited to meals with his family and even on family holidays. Outside the classroom he proved a rumbustious older brother to many; if some held him in awe, as they undoubtedly did, it was not a deliberate cult on his part. He called the boys 'fellows', their own name for themselves. When teaching the sixth (his own form) in the room above the school gates, he sat on a plain kitchen chair, at a table on a level with theirs, not lecturing from the teacher's dais common at the time. Unusually for the time he would always admit when he did not know the answer and try to learn with his class. Mere cleverness he did not admire, likening it to the cleverness of lawyers divested of moral character with conviction or acquittal, not truth, as the aim. He admired the plodder rather than the genius to whom learning came easily. Education to Arnold was fundamentally the religious and moral training of character. Every lesson he taught began with prayer, preceded by silence as Arnold glanced round to see that all were suitably seriously inclined. He had a manner of 'awful reverence' when speaking of God or of the Scriptures (Stanley, 1844, 1845 edition: 32) and there was a feeling that 'when his eye was upon you, he looked into your inmost heart' (ibid.: 184). 'The depth of his tones, and the pathos of his voice [reading Wordsworth] still linger in the chambers of memory ... Under his vivid teaching, the rolling eloquence and grand prophetic inspiration of Deuteronomy grew into one's soul, spite of struggling through it in the crabbed [Septuaguint] Greek' (Gover, 1895: 36). The power and presence of 'the Doctor' (Arnold received his DD in 1828) was awesome. Even Stanley admits a 'peculiar vehemence in language' (1844, 1845 edition: 198) in speaking of contemporary events, 'an unhasting, unresting diligence' (ibid.: 234).

Adolescence was to Arnold a time of trial and temptation between the idyll of childhood and the maturity of adulthood. There was plenty of evidence in contemporary behaviour in public schools to illustrate this, from cases of homosexual rape (boys still slept six to a bed in some schools in the 1820s), to bullying including roasting 'fags' (junior boys), extortion, gambling, alcohol excess, riding to hounds, poaching, attacking local residents and other illicit activities. Arnold's radical solution was to reduce adolescence to a minimum, by expecting adult behaviour and trust among adolescents, especially older ones, and by curbing excesses when they did arise by firm but fair discipline. Boarding establishments, by removing parental influence, could themselves in Arnold's view harm adolescent boys. This was highly plausible in the pre-railway era of his early years at Rugby. Until railways made shorter terms practicable, the school year was divided into Long Half (twenty-one weeks from early February to late June) and Short Half (sixteen weeks from early August to late December), a two-term year.

Arnold and 'religious education' (spiritual development)

It is possible, from the sermons and the way in which Arnold structured Rugby School, to reconstruct his view of spiritual development. He called it 'religious education' and it is important not to confuse his usage with the twentieth-century name for the classroom subject: 'None can be more sensible than ourselves to the worthlessness of mere intellectual advancement, unless superintended by that Discipline which invariably combines the enlargement of the Understanding with the gradual correction and improvement of our moral nature' (unpublished essay, 1826, two years before he went to Rugby). For him a Christian school is a 'temple of God', although just like the Jerusalem Temple it can be corrupted and can then harm its members, e.g. by condoning drunkenness or bullying or lying. Individual members have a duty towards the school. They are not there to please themselves. In some schools hatred of authority, general idleness and peer pressure to behave badly are the very opposite of Christian love. Set in this context, the male community of the boys' public school under Arnold became a sort of Christian monastery, with Chapel at the heart and with all its teaching religious in intention. By 1839 prayers were held daily at 7 a.m. and 7.45 p.m.; on Sundays they were held at 8.30 a.m. and 7.45 p.m. with first Chapel from 11 a.m. to 12 noon and second Chapel from 4 p.m. until approximately 5 p.m. Sundays also brought an hour's learning of a gospel passage after breakfast, and sometimes a psalm, and an hour after lunch to prepare three or four Bible chapters for the Second Lecture held from 3 p.m. to 4 p.m. In School House, which Arnold headed, the night prayer was read by a praepostor after a reading by Arnold himself in English, translating from his Greek Testament.

Arnold was very much aware of the difficulties faced by all schools: 'This common and well known Feature of a School—its Roughness, Coarseness, Want of Feeling, to say nothing of its positive Unkindness and Spirit of Annoyance, does this bear any Resemblance to the Temper of those who are the inhabitants of the Kingdom of God? (Sermon on Psalm 94.2, 27 November 1836). Teachers should not be in the old master–slave relationship but should be like parents. Their example can be crucial. 'Religious education' is to enable children to reach out to life eternal, 'making them know and love God, know and abhor evil ... teaching our understandings to know the highest truth ... the highest good' (*Sermons*, 1842: 88). Can teachers accomplish this great task? Is it impossible? In commercial schools the religious teaching varies probably more than anything else, according to the personal character of the instructor. It is not like teaching the three Rs, but the catechism, the words of hymns and the 'great truths of the gospel' provide a 'map of the road' (ibid.: 184). The curriculum has to allow proper space for this development. Physical science cannot instruct the judgement. Only moral and religious knowledge can accomplish this. Teaching history, moral and political philosophy with no reference to the Bible is not possible without giving children an anti-religious education. Arnold recognised no middle ground. Curriculum was either religious or, by the absence of religion, anti-religious. 'I cannot reject from religious education whatever ministers to the perfection of our bodies and our minds, so long as both in body and our mind, in soul and spirit, we ... may be taught to minister to the service of God' (Sermons, 1834: 208).

But this sort of education is effected by the whole school community, not merely lessons. The characteristics of childhood include experience of temptations, being 'slaves to present influences' (neither looking backwards nor forwards to interpret the present situation), and being unfit to guide themselves (Sermons, 1844: 14). Children, after the innocence of early childhood is lost, are ignorant and selfish, living only for the present. Arnold believed that adolescence in children in attitudes and behaviour corresponded to the adolescence of the human race. Adolescents needed the claims of Christianity setting before them clearly and uncompromisingly. It was a mistake to appeal to the reason of the child in a situation where obedience should be required. Children are 'under the law' (I Timothy 1.9) and therefore require a system with rules, disciplines and, where necessary, punishments. Without that, childhood innocence could be corrupted by adolescents into hardness, coarseness, cruelty and stupidity. Corporal punishment for boys is neither degrading, nor unchristian *per se*. It must not be too excessive nor too frequent, nor must it be applied to older boys. Fagging and the use of praepostors (prefects), properly controlled, regulates what would otherwise be the impossibility of equality between different year groups of children. Addressing the members of the Rugby Mechanics' Institute in 1838, Arnold urged that 'a docile and yet enquiring mind best becomes us both as men and as Christians' (*Miscellaneous Works*, 1845: 424).

In an often-quoted dictum referred to above, Arnold remarked that he wanted to produce Christian *men*, for Christian *boys* he could not hope to make. There were a few positive aspects of childhood. They included that children were very teachable (and therefore needed good examples) and that the transition to adulthood could be hastened. This phase was marked when a time of 'principle' was attained, potentially in the sixth-form years. Those not entering the sixth missed the high point and climax of the whole education process. Arnold's own character was consistent with this. Whitridge (1928: 90) sums it up as a passionate belief in Christ; a hatred of sin; an unswerving sense of conduct; the conviction that education could not thrive without Christianity; and that mental cultivation is properly a religious duty.

> He made us understand that the only thing for which God cares ... is goodness, that the only thing which is supremely hateful to God is wickedness. All other things are useful, admirable, beautiful in their several ways. All forms, ordinances, means of instruction, means of amusement, have their places in our lives ... In his view, there was no place or time from which Religion is shut out, there is no place or time where we cannot be serving God by serving our fellow-creatures. (Stanley, 1874: 1)

Arnold's legacy

> Watch ye stand fast in the faith. Quit you like men. Be strong.
> (Inscription at the base of the statue of Thomas Hughes at Barby Road, Rugby)

The statue whose inscription is quoted above was unveiled by Frederick Temple, himself a Rugby head in the style of Arnold, who went on to become Archbishop of Canterbury. Arnold provided a model for schooling that later Victorian educators were happy to espouse, the school as a Christian community, with education as a Christian mission. He endorsed it in a personal role model. It was not always evident to later Victorian critics of Arnold that he stood within an unbroken family tradition of Christianity which made it easier to adopt this position. His children Jane, Tom and Matt endured a perhaps more typical later Victorian loss or at least reformulating of faith in a climate in which increasingly people had to find a faith for themselves. His son William, as director of public instruction in a newly founded department, reformed the Punjab education system, but died at 31 while returning invalided to the UK. Arnold's three main aims as head of Rugby had been to inculcate, in descending order, religious and moral principles; gentlemanly conduct; and intellectual ability. To this he added massive energy devoted to work—as sixth-form teacher, head, chaplain, historian, correspondent with many old boys—and devoted to his family. The later Arnold myth is partly accountable for by the fact that he lived out the work and moral ethic that many later Victorians came to emulate. Some of his leading pupils became influential heads a generation on: Benson at Wellington; Butler at Haileybury; Cotton and Bradley at Marlborough; Gell in Van Diemen's Land (Tasmania); Lee at King Edward's, Birmingham; Vaughan at Harrow.

There was a second-generation influence. T.W. Jex-Blake is a clear example of Arnoldian influence, although he never knew Arnold personally. As a boy he was destined for Eton, but when his father read Stanley's *Life of Arnold* (1844, 1845 edition), he was deeply impressed and 'told me that he had no idea that any school attempted to act on the X$_{an}$ [Christian] ideal' (in Simpson, 1967: 102). Jex-Blake was sent to Rugby instead. After a double First at Oxford and a short spell at Marlborough, he taught at Rugby from 1857 to 1868, moving to the headship of Cheltenham and returning to Rugby as head from 1874 to 1887, defeating Temple's nominee, the redoubtable John Percival, who in the event succeeded him.

Arnold died suddenly, on the eve of his forty-seventh birthday, at the end of his fourteenth year at Rugby. Characteristically, on the evening before, he had hosted an end of term supper for sixth-form boys in his House. His last private diary entry illustrates the earnestness which his opponents so derided and his supporters admired:

> The day after tomorrow is my birthday, if I am permitted to live to see it ... How large a portion of my life on earth is already passed. And then—what is to follow this life? How visibly my outward work seems contracting and softening into the employments of old age ... Still there are works which, with God's permission, I would do before the night cometh ... But above all, let me mind my own personal work,—to keep myself pure and zealous and believing,—labouring to do God's will, yet not anxious that it should be done by me rather than by others, if God disapproves of my doing it. (ibid.: 333f.)

Arnold was buried under the altar in the school chapel. He had combined the earnestness of the evangelical, a catholicity of churchmanship which was rarely equalled before the twentieth-century ecumenical movement, a willingness to confront the gospel with modernity well in advance of most of his contemporaries, social concern that extended beyond the children of the comfortably off, scholarship in history and theology, effective and memorable classroom teaching, active pastoral care, personal religious devotion and a vision of education with Christianity at the centre, not the periphery. He was not to find an equal and his influence on the public schools and on their twentieth-century imitators, the grammar schools, was immense. Despite Strachey and the decline of Victorian moral idealism, Arnold's legacy in English education was not finally eclipsed until the vastly changed social and religious landscape of the 1960s and the gradual disappearance of most of the grammar schools. Even his views on the educational benefits of giving power to praepostors (prefects) vanished in the sixth forms of comprehensive schools, where a new emphasis on egalitarianism meant that either the prefectorial system was abandoned, or all sixth formers were made prefects and the status and role of the office was reduced.

When Stanley spoke at Rugby thirty-two years after Arnold's death, it was fitting that he quoted the passage read in Chapel on the Sunday after Arnold's death, Samuel's farewell reminder (I Samuel 12.2) that his sons were with the people. His last head boy referred to Arnold's extraordinary sense of the reality of the invisible world. Arnold could see the spiritual as well as the moral. Arnold's supporters told his critics that his system of education was not *based* on religion; it *was* religion (Wymer, 1953: 171).

Some of his pupils—Arthur Hugh Clough and Arnold's own sons Matthew and Thomas, for instance—found Arnold at times overpowering, although this view has been challenged (Wymer, 1953; Trevor, 1973). Lesser heads tried to cultivate something similar for generations and often tried to present themselves in this light in the only activity that brought the whole school together: worship. The problem was that to copy Arnold's actions without Arnold's passion and sense of purpose, the mind-set behind them, was not as easy as might appear. Frederick Temple's biographer said of him that he 'had no perception that a system which had worked well at Rugby, when controlled by himself, could scarcely be made the basis of a religious settlement under the conditions of party government' (Sandford, 1907: 94).

Nevertheless Arnold remains a crucial figure, probably the most crucial figure, in the development of the spiritual in UK schooling for five reasons: he adapted and channelled some of Coleridge's seminal thinking into the practical business of running a school; his headteacher imitators, however inferior, were numerous and influential; the Hughes–Stanley cult portrait proved both enduring and influential (Hughes's opening, set in the Vale of the White Horse, Berkshire, also appealed widely to a nostalgia for the vanishing 'Merrie England' and was captured in Matthew Arnold's *Scholar Gypsy* of 1853); the Arnold dynasty continued to exercise an influence on national education, notably through Matt ('Crab') and Jane ('K'), and overseas in the brief work of Tom in Van Dieman's Land and William in the Punjab, as well as in former pupils who became heads; and finally Arnold himself was a serious thinker and writer who deserves to be seen as much more than a Titan personality.

Matthew Arnold (1822–1888)

Matthew Arnold, recognised as a high-profile poet and *litterateur,* was also an inspector of schools from 1851 to 1886. One commentator sees him as caught between the aesthetic and the anthropological, his Oxford Professorship of Poetry and his grinding school inspection work (Eagleton, 1998). It meant that like his father, his views on the place of the spiritual in education were based on encounters with real children, in Matthew's case across a very wide sample of schools, though with a nonconformist predominance. In some ways he reacted against his father (cultivating a foppish appearance and manner at Oxford; in his narrative poem *Sohrab and Rustum* a mighty father unconsciously kills his son; Matthew makes no reference in his educational writing to his father's work; nor did he send his own sons to Rugby but instead to Harrow as day boys). In other ways he inherited his father's seriousness, sense of purpose and public mission. His poems are often melancholy, falling back on stoic consolation. Water and moonlight are recurring images. *Rugby Chapel* (1857) is an elegiac poem in memory of Thomas Arnold. It finds Matthew significantly outside the church rather than inside, on a gloomy autumn evening in the Close. He recalls his father's 'radiant vigour', 'buoyant cheerfulness' and sheltering spirit. Thomas is referred to as unwearied, upraising with zeal the 'humble good' and sternly repressing the bad.

Matthew lacked Thomas's explicitly Christianising vision for education, seeing danger in denominational-sponsored education in that it might be used to promote religious authority instead of the liberal culture of the human spirit. He was also conscious that many people perceived that the time of the Christian religion was passing:

> The millions suffer still, and grieve,
> And what can helpers heal
> With old-world cures men half believe
> For woes they wholly feel?
> (*Obermann Once More*, 1867, verse 59)

But Matthew Arnold had not passed into full agnosticism. His wife described him as 'a good Christian at bottom' (in Chambers, 1947: 104), and like many of his contemporaries Arnold accepted the moral framework of Christianity, a view that was to transpose and dilute into the twentieth-century popular view that the religious presence in curriculum matters because it teaches children 'right from wrong'. Matthew Arnold developed a view of 'culture', not as a mere residuum of heritage to which children should be introduced, but as a living tradition of values with a moral, social and beneficent character, which was in conflict with a baser value-set, 'Philistinism'. Education was seen as a battle between the protagonists of both sets of values in which Arnold wished to see culture prevail.

> [An] irresistible force ... is gradually making its way everywhere, removing old conditions and imposing new, altering long-fixed habits, undermining venerable institutions, even modifying national character: the modern spirit ... Yes, the world will soon be the Philistines'! ... and the whole earth filled and ennobled every morning by the magnificent roaring of the young lions of the *Daily Telegraph*, we shall all yawn in one another's faces with the dismallest, the most unimpeachable, gravity ... How it has augmented the comforts and conveniences of life for us! Doors that open, windows that shut, locks that turn, razors that shave, coats that wear, watches that go, and a thousand more good things, are the invention of the Philistines. (in Gribble, 1967: 52, 74, 85)

Saintsbury notes that in a single year, 1852, Arnold's inspection district included Lincoln, Nottingham, Derby, Stafford, Salop, Hereford, Worcester, Warwick, Leicester, Rutland, Northants,

Gloucester, Monmouth, the whole of south Wales and much of north Wales, with some schools in the East and West Ridings of Yorkshire. He travelled mostly by railway. But these inspections were limited to nonconformist schools and this coloured Arnold's view of Philistinism, which was derived from the worst excesses of Dissent. 'We must never forget that for nearly twenty years Mr Arnold worked in the shadow, not of Barchester Towers, but of Salem Chapel' (Saintsbury, 1902: 48). Margaret Oliphant's *Salem Chapel* (1863) was indeed a caustic fictional treatment of some aspects of Dissent in a petty-minded, small-town setting.

In the course of his enquiries into education abroad, Matthew produced reports which provoked considerable discussion about education in the UK. As an inspector he also had to test pupil-teachers, mark examinations, question children, and conduct enquiries with school managers. In 1855 he inspected 117 'institutions', 173 schools, 368 pupil-teachers and 97 certificated teachers (Murray, 1996: 148). Pressure of work was intense; in 1868 he stayed up till 4 a.m. at the death bed of his son Basil, reading examination scripts, and later the same year was writing the preface to *Culture and Anarchy* at the death bed of his son Tommy. Although he found much of his inspectorial role to be drudgery, not least the incessant travel and absences from home, by his stringent criticism of so much of what he saw in schools as encouraging mechanical and unimaginative teaching methods and a low conception of the role of the teacher he produced an implicit philosophy for education: 'Sewing, calculating, writing, spelling are necessary; they have utility, but they are not formative. To have the power of reading is not in itself formative ... Good poetry is formative; it has too the precious power of acting by itself and in a way suggested by nature' (in Fitch, 1897: 183). Letters, poetry and religion were seen by him as antidotes to too scientific a curriculum.

> Not milder is the general lot
> Because our spirits have forgot,
> In action's dizzying eddy whirl'd,
> The something that infects the world.
> ('Resignation', 1849, 275–8)

He was prepared to risk the wrath of his superiors in presenting reports which were sharply critical of mechanistic assumptions about education. As a lay inspector he could not inspect Church of England schools, but saw much of Wesleyan and British and Foreign Schools Society schools. He saw Bible teaching as an important source for intellectual, moral and religious stimulus and regretted that denominational controversy (which had removed it from government inspection) had probably weakened its status in schools. The God of the Bible is simply and solely 'the Eternal Power, not ourselves, that makes for righteousness, by which all things fulfil the law of their being'. Arnold noted that the Bible engages 'feelings and imagination' and for the elementary school child is almost their only contact with poetry and philosophy (Fitch, 1897: 195, 197). He was also aware of the difficulties of articulating spirituality, on his forty-first birthday writing: 'I can feel … an inward spring which seems more and more to gain strength, and to promise to resist outward shocks … But of this spring one must not talk, for it does not like being talked about, and threatens to depart if one will not leave it in mystery' (in Chambers, 1947: 128). He addressed this again in *Culture and Anarchy*:

> To the many who think that spirituality, and sweetness, and light, are all moonshine, this [a vocational view of education] will not matter much; but with us, who value them, and who think that we have traced much of our present discomfort to the want of them, it weighs a great deal … [The operation of culture is] an inward spiritual activity, having for its characters increased sweetness, increased light, increased life, increased sympathy. (in Gribble, 1967: 98, 112f.)

These could be 'vacuous, high-minded pieties' (Eagleton, 1998: 22), a thread of criticism that could be levelled at much twentieth-century discourse on the spiritual in education. But despite his aversion to over-formulating the spiritual, Matthew Arnold was perhaps nearer to a more systematised expression of Coleridge's scattered thoughts on education than to Thomas Arnold's. But he and his father had common ground in agreeing that character-building in education matters more than knowledge; that religious and moral training is supremely important, but not to be equated with instruction in formularies and creeds; that reverence for the past can enhance life in the present; that activities to engender a noble and intelligent life matter more than those simply to lead to a job. As the superstitious elements of religion declined, as Arnold believed they must, increasing trust would be placed in science; hence it was essential for a new humane framework of belief to be developed. Without using much explicit vocabulary about the spiritual, Matthew Arnold nevertheless asserted a spiritual as well as aesthetic and humane base for a philosophy of education. He also attended to the notion of development: 'The human race has the strongest, most invincible tendency to *live*, to *develop* itself. It retains, it clings to what fosters its life ... to the literature which it exhibits in its vigour' (in Murray, 1996: 158, Arnold's italics). The problem faced by teachers (Arnold saw this only too well as an inspector) was a strikingly modern one: to define what this meant in practice and then to find time to apply it within a system which in practice prioritised other goals. He found pupil-teachers to be too much filled with facts and lamentably short of 'culture', the classical and literary background which was both character-forming and humanising (Murray, 1996: 126f.). Culture as an understanding of the best that has been thought and said in the world, used as a critique of current assumptions, should be open to all. At some professional risk he attacked the government moves towards payment by results, arguing that schools were in danger of becoming machines for teaching reading, writing and arithmetic rather than communities with complex functions, religious, moral and intellectual.

Matthew Arnold was not, as a misreading of 'Dover Beach' (1867) suggested to some, an agnostic. He remained a worshipping believer, albeit to many an unorthodox one, all his life. He opposed 'idolaters with a Bible-fetish' and their 'horribly absurd dogmas' (Murray, 1996: 256). He brought little sustained discussion to the notion of spirituality in education. But in his concept of culture, his non-sectarian views of religious teaching, his aesthetic and humane approach to what schooling should be about, and by authority derived from his inspectorial work, this Arnold added a unique contribution to the values debate about the UK curriculum and the place of the spiritual within it. When Thomas Arnold brought an immense force of personal conviction to his view, he could not easily be imitated because he personified the ethos of Rugby in his time. Without him Rugby could not be, and never was, the same, even under imitators. Matthew too had his personal convictions, partly derived from an immense breadth of experience of what was actually happening in schools across the country and an awareness that education must take into account a rapidly changing and increasingly technological society, not merely in its implications for information explosion, but in the ethical and moral issues being raised and the need to provide for the spiritual as well as the material. Matthew's convictions were no less real than his father's, but less dependent on personality to uphold them. They have proved more durable in the development of attitudes to the spiritual in the UK educational system and more relevant to an industrialised society promoting mass education.

The rise of an agnostic spirituality

Matthew Arnold can be regarded as a bridge between the confident Christian educational vision of a pre-Victorian and early Victorian age, as typified by his father, and the later and more modern plural views that embrace a less confident Christianity (in the twentieth century complemented by other religions) alongside agnostic and atheist views of varying degrees of sympathy towards notions of spirituality. Two Victorian case studies illustrate well how the agnostic and Deist strands of spirituality developed. They were to become dominant in educational thinking in the twentieth century as Christianity became increasingly to be perceived as one religion among many and, in the UK, a declining one at that. Many more exemplars of the rise of an agnostic spirituality could be added. The omnipresent Thomas Arnold re-appears, briefly, in both of them.

Mary Arnold's *Robert Elsmere* (1888)

Mary Augusta Ward (1851–1920), Mrs Humphry Ward as she preferred to be known after her marriage, was a grand-daughter of Thomas Arnold by his son Thomas ('Tom'), whose conversion to Roman Catholicism, return to the Church of England and reconversion to Roman Catholicism were to cause his wife and dependants considerable uncertainty, dislocation of accommodation and income, and personal distress. Tom had married on the Doctor's birthday, 13 June 1850, while working in the education service in Van Diemen's Land (Tasmania). Returning to England destitute as a result of Tom's first conversion to Roman Catholicism and consequent loss of job, Mary (then five) was left by her parents at Fox How under the charge of her grandmother,

Mary Arnold senior, the Doctor's widow, and an unmarried aunt, Frances Arnold (Aunt Fan), while her father went to Dublin in search of work with J.H. Newman.

Mary was a difficult child, whose tantrums were to become legendary, and she was packed off to Ambleside to a school run by Anne Clough, sister of the Rugbeian poet, Arthur. Mary never entirely recovered from the grinding poverty of these years and the effectual abandonment of her by her parents. She was eventually reunited with them in Oxford in 1867, where her sisters Ethel and Julia had been in their childhood among the female photographic subjects befriended by Rugbeian Charles Dodgson (Lewis Carroll). Mary started to write in 1869.

If Mary inherited the Arnold forcefulness of personality, she also possessed their sense of high moral purpose, as an active philanthropist, supporter of women's entry to higher education and yet as a high-profile opponent of women's suffrage. *Robert Elsmere* was her best-known of six novels and one of a growing type such as J.A. Froude's *The Nemesis of Faith* (1849), which attempted to explore what remained after a loss of orthodox Christian faith. Ward's novel was written against an extremely difficult recent personal background: Mary's mother, Julia, was suffering from breast cancer; her difficult brother Arthur had been killed in the Basuto war (1878); her agnostic mentor, Mark Pattison, died in 1884; and her own problematic health culminated in a physical breakdown in 1886–7. *Robert Elsmere* occupied three years of writing: from March to November 1885 she was planning it; from November 1885 to March 1887 she was writing it; from March 1887 to January 1888 she was revising it, principally to make it shorter. The first draft was reckoned at 1,358 pages in printed form and truncation was demanded by the publisher, Smith Elder.

Volume I is set in the Lake District and tells the story of Catherine Leyburn's dilemma, whether to accept her suitor Robert Elsmere or whether to follow the call of duty and continue to look after her widowed mother at home. In Volume II Elsmere, now Rector of Murewell in Surrey, is in dialogue with the agnostic squire, Roger Wendover. His old Oxford heroes, Edward Langham and Mr Grey, are also involved in the contest for Robert's soul, on the side of the growing cultured scepticism. Grey, based on T.H. Green, argues a philosophy based on a mixture of Christianity, scepticism and social action. Mary Ward cut most of

Robert's speeches in defence of Anglicanism, thus leaving the debate unbalanced and his character enfeebled. Volume III follows Robert after his loss of orthodox faith into the slums of London, where he is involved in a new religious community, but when the novel ends with his death, there is some ambivalence as to whether his spiritual journey has been a victory or a defeat. The book finally appeared less than two months before the death of Mary's mother and of 'Uncle Matt', who had collapsed and died of a heart attack in Liverpool.

Robert Elsmere was an instant success. It outsold Darwin massively. Gladstone wrote a review of it. Smith Elder were immediately required to produce reprints. Seventeen editions of the one-volume form of the novel appeared between July 1888 and September 1889, 38,000 copies in all. It was pirated in the USA where an estimated 100,000 copies were sold within six months. It made the career and guaranteed the financial security of its author for life. Yet it is a badly written book, with an improbable story line and some tedious and occasionally melodramatic sub-plots. Why did it succeed, where better novels failed? The answer must lie in its appeal to a public which was moving away from confidence in institutional religion, but not ready for atheism.

At Oxford, Elsmere had 'a young and roving curiosity' (I, 1888: 99) and an earnestness befitting Arnoldian Rugby (ibid.: 112). His hero, Mr Grey, had declined ordination as he rejected miracles, but his influence did not deter Elsmere from ordination, nor from marrying a devout, utterly orthodox evangelical, Catherine. For Elsmere's other Oxford influence, Langham, orthodox Christianity 'at the first honest challenge of the critical sense withers in our grasp!' (ibid.: 357). At Murewell, Elsmere's early defence against Squire Wendover allows the squire modern scholarship and cynicism on his side, pitted against only the world's humble seekers (II, 1888: 91). It is hardly an even match, as Wendover is revealed to be a researcher and writer, having been working on one project on the nature of religious evidence for thirty years, and is revealed as having achieved a doctorate in Berlin, seat of German theological heresy in the eyes of orthodox English church people. Moreover Wendover has full time for study, which Elsmere is denied. The Christian story, to Wendover, had its origins dependent on a place and time now gone for ever. In such a time it would be surprising if Jesus were not noted as performing miracles; the East was full of Messiahs; Nero is believed to survive death. So the Resurrection 'is partly invented, partly imagined, partly ideally true—in any case wholly intelligible and natural, as a product of the age, when once you have the key of that age' (ibid.: 247). To Wendover, Roman Catholicism is dead as an intellectual force, and western Protestantism is 'the most sterile hybid in the world' (ibid.: 215). Elsmere's intellectual fascination with the squire deprived Catherine of his time and company and eventually created a barrier between them. But Elsmere lacked the time and energy to fight Wendover intellectually (and many of his speeches were cut out in the final editing process) and he was gradually and inevitably won over. He did believe in God, in Jesus as a teacher, a martyr, in the idea of Christ as 'the world's eternal lesson'(ibid.: 325) that God is in all people. This was devastating for Catherine, and Robert resigned his living on principle. Wendover is only briefly challenged strongly—'had he ever grasped the meaning of religion to the religious man?' (ibid.: 372)—and at one other point in the plot when he appears to have an overwhelming experience of being haunted, the supernatural ending of Volume II.

But for Elsmere it was not strictly a loss of faith at all, but a reformulation. 'After the crash, *faith* [Ward's italics] emerged as strong as ever, only craving and eager to make ... a fresh compact with the reason' (III, 1888: 39). Catherine continued to occupy the old ground: 'if the Gospels are not true in fact, as history, as reality, I cannot see how they are true at all, or of any value' (ibid.: 35). Elsmere ended working in the New Brotherhood, a cross between a Labour church and a university settlement, with pictures of the Buddha, Socrates, Moses, Shakespeare, Paul and Jesus on the walls. He asserted his belief in God, conscience, experience and eternal goodness (ibid.: 201), quoting Matthew Arnold unacknowledged (*Obermann Once More*, ibid.: 209). The Brotherhood benediction is 'go in peace, in the love of God, and in the memory of his servant Jesus' (ibid.: 363). Elsmere died after great suffering and devotedly nursed by Catherine to the end. His dying words stemmed from a reminiscence of the birth of their first child and his joy that her pain was over. It was nothing like an orthodox Christian death bed repentance and return to the fold. The Brotherhood continued to grow, and his widow supported his charitable efforts, but continued in her own church and on the subject of his beliefs remained silent.

Novels may create climates of thought and they may also echo them. That such a badly written and long novel to read, even in its final form, proved so popular must lie in the themes which it was handling. It was a major marker that the public mood, or the mood of those who read novels, found fascinating the transition from the faith that the churches seemed to be promoting into an intellectually freer climate, in which belief in God was still assumed, but the right of the individual to determine their personal religious beliefs and observances was asserted. It was not for many a form of materialistic atheism. If it was less confident than orthodox Christianity sounded, it was at least as sincere. If it was not religious, it could claim to be spiritual. It was a form of spirituality without institutional religion and in the twentieth century, as it developed further, it became highly influential in the idea of 'spiritual development'. As the churches became more marginal it might even appear as the new orthodoxy, without acknowledging its Victorian roots.

The Arnoldian transition into a more agnostic environment did not end with Mary. Her sister Julia (1862–1908) married Leonard Huxley, son of T.H. Huxley. Aldous was their third child. Nor did the Arnoldian association with education end with Matt and Tom. Tom's daughter Lucy married Carus Selwyn, who went on to become head of Uppingham School. But the new mood that was to affect twentieth-century understanding of the spiritual existed well beyond the Arnold dynasty. In Rutherford it developed not against the context of the Church of England, but of nonconformity.

Mark Rutherford (1831–1913)

Mark Rutherford was the pen name of William Hale White. *The Autobiography* (1881) and *The Deliverance* (1885) [1927] of Mark Rutherford are, despite their titles, novels, although there is an autobiographical element in them. The style of writing is simple and powerful and compensates for plotting deficiencies. White grew up in Bedfordshire nonconformity and went to Cheshunt College, then to New College, St John's Wood, to train for the Independent (Congregational) ministry. His doubts about the literal interpretation of the Bible and traditional Christian doctrine, especially Calvinism, coupled with belief in a more mystical approach derived from Caleb Morris, Tennyson and Wordsworth and a reading of biblical commentators like Thomas

Arnold (still reckoned as unorthodox), led to his being expelled from the college. A job as a publisher's assistant, in which capacity he met George Eliot, was followed by work at Somerset House and in various posts in the Admiralty. In 1856 he 'supplied' (i.e. preached regularly during a period of ministerial vacancy) the pulpit of Ditchling Unitarian Chapel, Sussex. It was his last real church link and if Ditchling is the congregation of seventeen described in *Autobiography* in the town of 'D—', their retreat from Christian doctrine had left them in religious isolation and spiritual torpitude. Only the shopkeeper's wife in the congregation is commended for being 'generous, spiritual, and possessed of an unswerving instinct for what is right' (*Autobiography*, 1881: 188). The ideal of an intellectually active and questioning minister was not an acceptable one for small-town nonconformity. White was caught between the newly public and confident sounding atheism, exemplified by the journalist Mardon in *Autobiography*, which he could not wholly share, and the dogmatism, as he perceived it, of the churches, which was equally unacceptable. Although fascinated by the Bible as a book, not as a rule for life or source of doctrine, White gave his children no teaching on it. His developing views were forged against the backcloth of his first wife's degenerative illness and his doubts, though never total rejection, concerning immortality.

To him 'the religious temper' was a gift like that for poetry or painting. It was not universal. Humankind has an upwelling spring of life, energy, love, and if it is not channelled, 'it turns the ground around it into a swamp' (in MacLean, 1955: 301). After a complete nervous breakdown, the Rutherford of *Autobiography* spends his Sunday mornings on the downs and lanes of Surrey admiring natural life, at peace with himself, content with incompleteness, happy 'to rest and wait' (*Autobiography*: 255), less anxious about death by virtue of loosening his anxiety for life. *The Deliverance* ends in autumn countryside, away from the oppressive tedium of work, not in sadness but joy and a sense of repose. 'We know that there is a great Power in existence, altogether friendly' (1885 [1927]: 165f.).

Perhaps in White are the seeds of some current perceptions of spirituality. Like Robert Elsmere, he has moved beyond the Christianity of the churches and beyond social or institutional religious forms and beliefs. Yet he has not moved into atheism; indeed atheism is just as unacceptable because of its dogmatic claims as churchgoing Christianity. This is also true for George Eliot. What Rutherford has is a reverence for life, a belief in God, although an unwillingness to say too much about God, and a social concern for the condition of humankind. He remains emphatically spiritual, not merely moral.

The Unitarian contribution

For many Victorians Unitarianism, with its renunciation of formal Christian dogma and creeds and its wide spectrum of belief, offered a half-way house between dogma and atheism. It also helped those who saw themselves as being fed by various of the world's great religions to achieve this within a homely and distinctively English cloak of nonconformity with chapels and ministers and the familiar paraphernalia inherited from the Presbyterian legacy of much English Unitarianism. As the era progressed, however, many passed from Unitarianism to no practice at all, or reverted to Unitarian services only for rites of passage, as in the case of the funerals of G.H. Lewes and his partner, 'George Eliot'. The continuing decline of Unitarianism in England in the twentieth century has tended to make its nineteenth-century contribution a neglected study. One case illustrates an emerging strand within the development of understanding of spirituality and that is the career of Moncure Conway (1832–1907).

Conway became the minister of South Place Chapel (Unitarian), Finsbury, in 1864. His predecessor, who had been in post for forty years, had proclaimed what was popularised as 'the Fatherhood of God and the Brotherhood of Man', with an emphasis on the latter. But he had gradually withdrawn from the chapel to involve himself in liberal reform as an MP from 1847. Conway, who had grown up in the USA under the influence of Methodist salvationism, then of Hicksite (mystical) Quakerism, finally becoming a Unitarian after reading the Hindu scriptures, became the next minister. He had shocked his Cincinnati congregation by defending scepticism, Eastern religions, Darwin and the theatre, while attacking orthodox Christianity in the form of the infallibility of the Bible and the atoning death of Jesus. At South Place he rapidly drew the leading literary doubters of London to his services, but he took its Unitarianism nearer to agnosticism: readings from world religions replaced the Bible; a semi-meditative monologue replaced prayer;

on one occasion an essay on William Blake and mysticism was the subject of the sermon, on another a passage from J.A. Froude's renunciation of Christianity was the source; non-Christian speakers were invited; the pulpit was known instead as 'the desk'; the text inscribed on the wall behind the minister was 'To thine own self be true'; among the names Conway recommended for inscription on the chapel walls were Jesus, Solomon, Zoroaster, Socrates, Buddha, Confucius, Plato, Muhammad, Omar Khayyam, Shakespeare, Spinoza, Bacon, Bruno, George Fox, Voltaire, Paine and Goethe. By 1876 Conway was recommending the replacement of Christianity by a higher view: Christ was not divine or even unique; his death was not an atonement; his miracles did not happen; he taught people to judge for themselves what is right, to pray in private not in churches; what is now posing as Christianity dates from the Council of Nicea; religions decay and become paganised; the divine life is manifest in 'the evolution of nature and the mystical movement in the heart of man' (in W.S. Smith, 1967: 117). Conway moved on from South Place in 1885 and it was not long before South Place Chapel became South Place Ethical Society and abandoned even its residual theism.

If Jesus was not unique, it is perhaps reassuring that neither was Conway. He typified a mood in Unitarianism and among other 'free thinking' congregations that was ready to dispense with the uniqueness and necessity of Christianity, first in favour of a liberal mixture of aspects of world religions and gradually in favour of the deification of evolution combined with the ideal of human progress, coupled with some residual ritual such as that adopted by the Positivist churches. It is strikingly similar to what is now being dispensed in some schools as 'spiritual development' and is a neglected area for research. It was to find some echo in the famous pastorate of Reginald Campbell at the City Temple from 1902: Jesus was an exemplar of goodness; goodness is a spirit rather than a code; 'Christ' is present in all people and in history.

In the twentieth century similar pilgrims' progresses were perhaps to be repeated by the many who had been sent to Sunday schools. But if they never graduated to adult church, neither did they graduate into atheism. The Pleasant Sunday Afternoon Movement (1875 onwards), 'Brief, Bright, Brotherly', a nonconformist-inspired endeavour to provide suitable but secular entertainment or education with a humanitarian slant for those who would not otherwise go to church, included a short prayer and a hymn or two as the religious element. It provides another uncanny parallel with a twentieth-century school curriculum which has a bit of worship tagged on. Both are easily susceptible to total secularisation and in both the spiritual element is truncated and isolated from the 'real' purpose of the event.

The beginning of the end of ideals

Thomas Arnold made Rugby different, but in many ways it remained a public school among public schools, and as the nineteenth century progressed it developed in some ways along with the rest. A Rifle Corps was established in 1860. After 1903 there was an Army Class in the school, which fed a steady stream of boys into Woolwich or Sandhurst. Three Rugbeian officers rode at the Charge of the Light Brigade; others were distinguished in the Indian Mutiny (two Victoria Cross awards), the Sikh, Burmese, Chinese, Afghan and South African Wars. The Great War was fed by Rugby men. At the outbreak in 1914 the entire school enlisted in the Rifle Corps. Of the 2,200 pupils admitted to the school by H.A. 'the Bodger' James during his tenure as head (1895–1910), 450 were killed. The final total of Rugbeian war dead numbered 686, more than the school's total number on roll at the end of the war.

Rupert Brooke (1887–1915) was a Rugbeian, son of W.P. 'Tooler' Brooke, himself a legendary Rugby housemaster, whose dog used to sit in the waste paper basket in his lessons. When 'Tooler' died tragically in 1910, Rupert took over the house for a term. Rupert Brooke had started writing poetry as a pupil at Rugby and continued in his Fabian days at Cambridge. He was influenced by the Romanticism of the 1890s but also by the new trend for metaphysical revival and the 'new realism'. Before the war he could capture nostalgia, metaphysical wit and the happiness of love, and 'The Old Vicarage, Grantchester', written in Berlin, dates from this period (1912). When war broke out he was commissioned in the Royal Naval Division and sent to Gallipoli. The five sonnets called collectively *1914* constitute his war poems. They are mellifluous and sentimental praises of love of country, patriotic self-sacrifice in a noble cause, and release from the petty preoccupations of peacetime (he had love affairs behind him in England and Tahiti). Had Brooke lived longer, he might have reached the disillusionment of Sassoon and Owen (Brooke's 1915 'Fragment' hints at this), but he saw little action except a brief engagement at the defence of Antwerp and, weakened by dysentery, he died on ship in the Aegean as a result of a mosquito bite which led to septicaemia. It was hardly glorious, even allowing for the midnight burial amid the olive groves of Skyros occasioned by his ship's scheduled early morning departure. But if Brooke sought to ennoble death, as in Sonnets III and IV, 'The Dead', he did not condone mass slaughter. Others were to make him appear to do so. Preaching to hundreds of war widows, parents and orphans in St Paul's on Easter Day 1915, Dean Inge read Brooke's Sonnet V, 'The Soldier', beginning:

> If I should die, think only this of me:
> That there's some corner of a foreign field
> That is forever England ...

He did not read 'The Fragment', in which Brooke observes fellow soldiers playing cards on the troopship approaching battle:

> I would have thought of them
> —Heedless, within a week of battle—in pity,
> Pride in their strength and in the weight and firmness
> And link'd beauty of bodies, and pity that
> This gay machine of splendour'ld soon be broken,
> Thought little of, pashed scattered ...

Inge's sermon, also made famous by its disruption by an anti-war protester, along with a fulsome obituary on Brooke by Churchill in *The Times* (26 April 1915), ensured that Brooke was 'canonised for the needs of the nation and used as an instrument to promote further slaughter' (Silkin, 1972: 69). In Brooke as a case study we can see in cameo the collision of establishment needs to justify the war, a move from Kipling-like beginnings toward public disillusionment, and the hint of an end of a benevolent, liberal view embracing a strand of spirituality that presumed that humankind was getting better, that progress was inevitable and beneficial, and that people might draw nearer the divine by a sort of osmosis. Such a view was far from Thomas Arnold's, but by 1914 his view of humankind and childhood had been left behind. This dominant liberal view led many young men from the public schools and beyond to their death in the trenches and it is perhaps worth noting that spiritualities, like religions, are not necessarily good. Brooke may have sensed this in an earlier poem, 'On the Death of Smet-Smet, the Hippopotamus Goddess' (1908), in its Chorus:

> She was so strong,
> But Death is stronger.
> She ruled us long;
> But Time is longer.
> She solaced our woe
> And soothed our sighing;
> And what shall we do
> Now God is dying?

Spirituality through mysticism: W.R. Inge (1860–1954)

While alternative and agnostic approaches to spirituality were developing on the late Victorian scene, 'orthodox' Christianity was not static. Indeed, any study of church history reveals that orthodoxy actually moves, a rather unsettling thought for some of the orthodox themselves. What was orthodox when Victoria ascended the throne in 1837 was not identical with what was orthodox at her death in 1901. The churches were becoming more plural in belief and liturgical practices and there was a growing dialogue between them. Moreover they were increasingly open to the biblical critical findings of scholars whose Christian credentials were acceptable. At the same time there was something of a revival in Christian mysticism, and this too was to contribute towards the complex view of spirituality that was emerging.

Inge lived his adult life through the end of the Victorian era and into the modern. He was a Fellow of Hertford College, Oxford (1889–1905), Vicar of All Saints, Knightsbridge (1905–7), Lady Margaret Professor of Divinity at Cambridge (1907–11) and Dean of St Paul's (1911–34). He had been a school teacher for five years (1883–8) in four different schools—Aldenham, Harrow, Winchester and Eton—the first three in temporary posts and the fourth at the school he had attended as a boy. They were not his happiest years as he had difficulty with class control, and in 1921 he became embroiled in national educational controversy for appearing to suggest in a newspaper article that there should not be scholarship opportunities for working-class children to enter universities.

Inge was a Platonist for whom God was the 'supreme value'. The Christian revelation 'puts the keystone in the arch' of Platonism. This Christian keystone was the doctrine of the Incarnation. In addition to Roman Catholicism and Protestantism, Inge distinguished a third version of Christianity, 'a spiritual religion', going back to Plato, Paul and John, being born again at the Renaissance. Its characteristics are a firm belief in absolute and eternal values, an open mind towards the discoveries of science, and 'a reverent and receptive attitude to the beauty, sublimity and wisdom of the creation as a revelation of the mind and character of the Creator' (in Fox, 1960: 167f.). The Good was the whole mind of God. Inge studied and practised mysticism, arguing in his Bampton Lectures (1899) that mysticism in the sense of the 'dim consciousness of the *beyond*' or 'obstinate questionings of sense and outward things' had been neglected in England (Inge, 1899: 5, his Italics). But his biographer points out that for Plato God was ambiguous, being used alongside 'the gods' and the Good (Fox, 1960: 162). By using Platonic language, Inge was importing some of the ambiguity and by endorsing the language of Plotinus that God was the First, the Absolute, the One, Fox argued that he was also getting near to God being the nothing (ibid.: 165).

Symbols tend to petrify or evaporate their subject and lose their religious content, but then comes 'a return to the fresh springs of the inner life', a revival of spirituality in the midst of formalism or unbelief (ibid.: 5). Quoting Proclus, Inge states that humankind has an organ or faculty for the discernment of spiritual truth which is as much to be trusted as the organs of sense. This is paralleled in Inge's contemporary Evelyn Underhill (1875–1941), herself a convert to Christianity and exponent of mysticism, for whom spiritual education does not put something into a child, but rather 'educes' what it already has, as part of its spiritual faculty (Underhill, 1927: 177, 186).

For Inge, whatever view of reality deepens our sense of the tremendous issues of life in the world is nearer the truth than any view which diminishes that sense. Beauty is the mediator between the good and the true (Inge, 1899: 323); only the great poets have glimpsed the spiritual background to what lies behind the abstractions of science. In 1899 he could write that at a time when people were rejecting the ideas of the infallible Church and the infallible Bible, this could lead them to the true fundamentals of spirituality, 'the religious consciousness itself'. The whole personality acting in accord is the facility for a spiritual awareness, not just the 'feeling' or 'heart'. This does not make every person their own prophet, priest, saviour, but they are part of a process of the Church as a living body and not merely a belief-system.

Goodness, Truth and Beauty bring their own satisfaction and possess a universal quality, which can transport people out of themselves. When the experience of them is past they can still delight and people feel better for it. They are 'holy ground' (Inge, 1930: 380). The Ideals of Platonism are to him essentially values, not unrealised ideals but facts understood in their ultimate significance. The growth of spiritual religion was independent of Christianity, although Christianity used Platonic and Neo-Platonic insights with ease, despite a tendency to turn it into bureaucracy and the persecution of those with differing views (Inge, 1926: 10f.). Inge also affirmed the beauty of the human body. He compared Jesus's love of nature with that of Wordsworth. The difference was that in his poetry, Wordsworth loved nature more than people (Inge, 1899: 316). Wordsworth was a 'natural Platonist', i.e. although he had not formally studied Plato, he had a feeling for the variety of the temporal world and an awareness of the invisible and eternal world behind it. Platonism is 'a sustained attitude to life founded on deep conviction—a practical philosophy or religion' (Inge, 1926: 69). Wordsworth demonstrated another Platonic exemplar: a passion for unifying all experience. Inge anticipated criticism of his mystical approach as escapism, self-deception, wishful thinking, auto-suggestion, arbitrariness etc. by commenting that although wariness of experiences one has not personally had is entirely proper, and that it is conceivable that self-deception may occur, 'if our highest and deepest experiences cannot be trusted, it is useless to seek for truth anywhere' (in Fox, 1960: 168).

Inge's popular style of writing made him one of the best-known clerics of his generation and his longevity prolonged his influence. He was never thought of as a major commentator on education. Nevertheless, his approach to spirituality influenced many who were involved in education. He is a reminder that the view of spiritual development which came to dominate from the 1960s might owe more to Platonism than Christianity. God and the

52

Good are blurred. Spiritual development is in one sense an attempt to unify curriculum experience, which in terms of teaching 'subjects' is palpably divided and partial. For Inge the aim of education should not be the knowledge of facts but of values, 'which are facts apprehended in relation to each other and ourselves ... The uncultivated man [is one who, although he] may know the price of everything, knows the value of nothing' (Inge, 1938: 291). But for Inge spirituality was not 'the secular creed which eliminates God and leaves only love to men as the foundation of ethics' (in Fox, 1960: 227).

Frederick Temple (1821–1902) and William Temple (1881–1944)

William Temple was the son of Frederick Temple. Frederick, who was nearly sixty when William was born, had been head of Rugby from 1857 to 1869 (see p. 32). Prior to that his experience had included work as Principal of Kneller Hall Training College for pupil-teachers and workhouse schoolmasters and work as an education inspector, mainly of training schools. When Frederick took over Rugby, with no prior experience of classroom teaching, numbers were falling and the school was drifting. Even allowing for a strongly hagiographical tendency in his main biographer, Frederick Temple re-Arnoldised Rugby with the old magic: he had Arnold's untiring haste, in his youth on one occasion walking the 48 miles from Oxford in a day to meet Arnold; he combined headship with chaplaincy; taught the sixth form himself; commenced sixth-form lessons with Arnold's own prayer; respected the boys as people; indulged in boyish games such as climbing the elms in the Close; showed commitment to the Rugby Mechanics' Institute; tried to live out Christian ideals and acquired something of a cult following among his pupils for whom his 'combination of absolute sympathy with strong will' (How, 1904: 203) made the latter palatable. He came the nearest to Arnold of his successors and his influence was to continue during his later period as governor, eventually chair of the governors of the school, until his death. Matthew Arnold was quoted as saying: 'Mr Temple, more than any other man whom I have ever known, resembles, to the best of my judgment, my late father' (in Sandford, 1906: 153). While at Rugby, also like Thomas Arnold, Frederick Temple had incurred controversy by his broad church sympathies, in his case the contribution of a piece, 'The Education of the World', in *Essays and Reviews* (1860). This controversy pursued him when he was appointed Bishop of Exeter in 1869, but it could not prevent his translation via London to Canterbury in 1897, in the succession after another former Rugby head, A.C. Tait. He had advised Forster on the 1870 Act and Temple's last public act was to speak in favour of the 1902 education bill in the Lords, where he collapsed mid-speech. He died shortly afterwards.

William Temple was thus born into the Arnoldian tradition of broad Anglican views (his father had also dallied with Tractarianism), a high concept of the national church and a keen concern for education (and death in harness). He was 'enveloped in an upper-class Anglican culture which still believed itself to be a permanent, necessary part of an English society which would lose its essential character if it were not Anglican' (Kent, 1992: 10). The Rugby tradition was also present in William. He was a pupil there and later wrote that Arnold 'clearly put character before brains as the aim of education, and made the senior boys his colleagues for accepting it' (in Iremonger, 1948: 14). As an undergraduate William was much influenced by the idealist philosopher Edward Caird (1835–1908), a leading Neo-Hegelian, who strengthened his conviction that there was a universal Purpose behind the world, and the active presence of a real Will. Caird maintained that the religious principle was a necessary element in consciousness and that Christianity, by virtue of overcoming the antithesis between the real and the ideal, was the absolute religion.

William was appointed to the headship of Repton School in 1910, leaving to become Rector of St James's Piccadilly in 1914, Canon of Westminster (1919), Bishop of Manchester (1921), Archbishop of York (1929) and Archbishop of Canterbury (1942). He was very much involved in the Workers' Educational Association and the Student Christian Movement. Temple was also greatly involved in national life (his *Christianity and Social Order* was a Penguin Special), in the developing ecumenical movement internationally, and in working with R.A. Butler in the settlement of church school issues in the 1944 Education Act (Copley, 1997: 21ff.). Here he was as passionate about raising the school leaving age to 16 as developing agreed syllabuses.

Temple regretted the inadequate equipment and large classes in many schools. His vision for schooling was part of a vision for a

Christian social order which would aim for 'the fullest possible development of individual personality in the widest and deepest possible fellowship' (Temple, 1942: 100) and he placed great emphasis on the corporate life of the school. He urged that Education was the most important department of the state and that without education of a very high quality, 'there can be no life worth defending' (Temple, 1917: 226). Before the child is old enough to reason, it should be placed in an environment that enables it to love spontaneously what is lovely and hate what is hateful. True judgement is formed before the emergence of reason. Therefore the logical element in religion must be developed out of the emotional element and not before it, because otherwise it would stifle enquiry and paralyse imagination. The child should learn from the school community to strive for success beyond the individual in the success of the house or the whole school. Training in such 'social membership' (ibid.: 237) ranks above intellectual training. Temple had imbibed sufficient of post-Arnold Rugby to see games as one fundamental element in developing the corporate life. But the aim of education is 'broadly spiritual' and the three aims of the spiritual life are Goodness, Truth and Beauty. 'It must always be insisted that these are ends in themselves' (ibid.: 241). The second of his six-point manifesto for a just society, written in wartime, was that 'Every child should have the opportunity of an education till years of maturity, so planned as to allow for his peculiar aptitudes and make possible their full development. This education should throughout be inspired by faith in God and find its focus in worship' (Temple, 1942: 99).

However, the Nazis were admitted to be highly successful promoters of the corporate lives of schools (ibid.: 93); what matters to Temple is the right sort of corporate life, one that fosters both individual development and world fellowship. The class war is one example of a breach in the fellowship. For Temple there is only one candidate for this double function of schooling which has values adequate to the task: Christianity. This means much more than Christian doctrine in the curriculum. It means regular corporate worship, a whole-school Christian atmosphere and community service for others. The periods of worship should bring to a focus 'what is the spirit of the whole school community' (ibid.: 93). For Temple all children are God's children and their environment exists at three levels: the sub-human, studied in the natural sciences; the human, studied in the humanities; and the super-human, studied in 'Divinity'. Temple was also able to see what others took longer to see, namely that a 'neutral' or secular curriculum was in fact a powerful potential indoctrinator into atheism: 'To be neutral concerning God is the same thing as to ignore Him ... If the children are brought up to have an understanding of life in which ... there is no reference to God, you cannot correct the effect of that by speaking about God for a certain period of the day' (in Iremonger, 1948: 571). It was a modified version of Arnold, and in the 1944 settlement Temple characteristically wanted this to be applied to all schools, rather than merely to concern himself with Anglican schools. Later critics felt that he had sold the pass on a distinctive Anglican spirituality in favour of a universal, but only broadly Christian, substitute. Whether they were right or not, the settlement certainly affected the development of spirituality in so-called state schools.

A complex pattern of development has been traced, from Arnold to William Temple, embracing broadly Christian elements, agnostic elements and, with decreasing importance, muscularly Christian elements. Rugby did not monopolise the field, but it led it at times and mirrors it constantly. Many more exemplars could have been provided, but they illustrate the same point: that spiritual development, like Christianity, was no longer a monochrome affair, but plural in its manifestations and meanings.

Chapter Two

The Political Process and the Legal Provision

The 1870 Education Act and provision for the spiritual

The rivalry of the denominational schools and the inability of the denominations to finance universal elementary education led to increasing state involvement, first in financial subsidy, then in inspection, then in provision of board schools alongside a continuing subsidy for denominational schools (see pp. 18ff). But the government did not wish to take sides in the denominational wrangles and much of the debate at the bill stages of the legislation was taken up with resolving what many speakers referred to as 'the religious difficulty'. The Act therefore stated:

> It shall not be required of any child being admitted into or continuing in ... [any elementary school receiving government funding] that he shall attend or abstain from attending any Sunday School, or any place of religious worship, or that he shall attend any religious observance or any instruction in religious subjects in the school or elsewhere ... 7.(1)

Religious instruction and religious observance (worship) were required to take place at the beginning or end of a school session and the timetable 'permanently and conspicuously fixed in every schoolroom' so that a child might be withdrawn by their parent without loss of other schooling. Inspectors were given the right to 'inquire into any instruction in religious subjects given at the school, or to examine any scholar therein in religious knowledge or in any religious subject or book' (7.(3)). The word spiritual does not appear in this Act, neither did it feature in the debate. But it was inherent in the term religious education as used then and there is evidence that some of the legislators hoped that the provision for religious teaching would enhance what later became called the spiritual development of children. If their hopes were for development in the spiritual, these were linked with hopes for development of the moral, and it is possible to see emerging seeds of the later notion of 'spiritual, moral, social and cultural development'.

W.E. Forster and the Arnold influence

W.E. Forster (1818–86) was brought up in a Quaker family near Bridport, Dorset, in circumstances of poverty. He received no elementary schooling himself but had some private tutorial help. He was sent to a Friends' school in Hornsey where he remained, studying seriously and hard, exhibiting stereotypically traditional nineteenth-century Quaker diligence and conscientiousness. Along with many other Friends in the early 1840s he shed the distinctive Quaker grey clothing and the use of 'Thee' and 'Thou' and blended more into society. 'In appearance tall, graceless, and hirsute, Forster looked as though he came from rough yeoman stock' (McCarthy, 1964: 114). In 1850, by then a successful worsted mill owner in Burley in Wharfedale, Yorkshire, he married Jane Arnold, daughter of Thomas. The marriage took place according to the rites of the Anglican church, her church. Marrying outside the Society of Friends still led to disownment (termination of membership) among Quakers, but Forster had already drifted from commitment to the Society. He was to become an undogmatic low church Anglican, on marriage very much joining the Arnold family rather than Jane joining his. Nicknamed 'K' by her father and family, Jane was the eldest and possibly favourite child of Thomas Arnold, his confidante in his later years. Certainly she imbibed much of his outlook on education.

In 1861 Forster became Liberal MP for Bradford on the retirement of leading Congregationalist mill owner Titus Salt and in 1868 he took on responsibility for education. The 'very real, though at first sight not obvious' Arnoldian connection was noted (Fitch, 1897: 153). Mrs Humphry Ward, the daughter of Arnold's son Thomas and therefore 'K's' niece, was in the Ladies Gallery when Forster made his speech about the bill. She later wrote: 'The scheme of the Bill was largely influenced by William Forster's wife, and through her by the conviction and beliefs of her father' (in

58

Wymer, 1953: 199). Another biographer (Reid, 1888: 264) notes of Forster that 'his admission into a family of such intellectual distinction as that of Dr Arnold insensibly widened his sympathies, and brought his mind into contact with ideas of which he had known comparatively little before'. This might be another eulogistic view of the Arnold clan but it was a fair comment on Forster. Reid was a friend of the family and Jane supplied him with source material. Forster's diary also reveals that Jane went over his speeches on education with him. Thus the concerns of Thomas Arnold senior about the education of the poor, in which he had involved himself in his early teaching days at Laleham, in subsequent campaigning and in Mechanics' Institute work at Rugby, were to be turned into law by his son-in-law. Matthew Arnold, who was himself a close brother to 'K', as a school inspector (see p. 37) and brother-in-law found mutual interests in common with Forster. Forster also got on well with William Arnold (see p. 32). Jane wrote that they had much in common in character: William [Arnold] had 'great charm and great nobility ... remarkable energy and ardour, and something of youthful vehemence' (in Reid, 1888: 317). The 'youthful vehemence' no doubt came from 'the Doctor'. After the premature deaths of William and his wife, the Forsters took their four orphaned children into their own family. The 'Arnoldites' as some unsympathetic contemporaries were to call them, proved a force that was influential on legislative provision as well as curriculum theory. Thomas and Matthew were both quoted in the debate (e.g. Hansard 1870, CC: 276, and 1870, CXCIX: 663). Forster also consulted Frederick Temple, then Bishop of Exeter, about the bill; in Temple there was also a strong Rugby connection (see p. 53).

Forster's view of the place of the spiritual in education

It was hardly surprising, granted his background and the contemporary climate in education, that Forster was committed as early as 1849 to the belief that the Bible and the teaching of religion must form part of any national system of education. He had established in his factory a school, which he regularly visited, for 'half timers', i.e. child employees. It used the pupil-teacher system. He was a member of the Royal Commission on Middle Class Schools (1864–7). Although almost immediately after his arrival as MP Forster was made President of the Board of

Education, this was not a Cabinet post and by the standards of a century later it was a low-status government job.

The debate behind the Act

Part of the impetus for the 1870 Act came from middle-class fears about gangs of young unschooled criminals, known as 'street Arabs', coupled with what would now be viewed as a naive optimism that education with its distinctive moral tone and sense of duty would reform them. Some pockets of non-schooling were larger than others; up to 80 per cent of West Midlands children were said to be unschooled. If education was seen as Christian by legislators, it was an expression of political commitment not so much to the propagation of Christian belief (which was held to be hard to define on account of the fierce denominational division), as to what passed for the Christian ethic in Victorian Britain, 'not so much a shining beacon toward which men and women might strive; it was more the bogey figure introduced when the police and the other forms of social cohesion seemed to be failing' (Midwinter, 1995: 69). Forster partially lends support to this view: 'The enormous majority of this country agrees, that the standard of right and wrong is based on religion, and that when you go against religion you strike a blow against morality' (in Reid, 1888: 488). To Charles Kingsley he wrote: 'I wish parsons, Church and *other* [his italics], would all remember as much as you do that children are growing into savages while they [the clergy] are trying to prevent one another from helping them'. Forster also addressed the vexed denominational question:

> [In extending school provision] it would not be fair to tax a Roman Catholic to teach Methodism ... It is not unfair to levy a rate on a Roman Catholic for the secular education of a Methodist ... If the rate payers give aid to any denominational schools, they should do so impartially; if to any, then to all efficient schools, whether denominational or secular. The religious difficulty ... will not be hard to overcome, if we remember, first, that we are and mean to remain a Christian people; and next, that we have made up our minds that the government shall not in any future legislation attempt to teach any special form of Christian faith. (Diary entry, 10 October 1869 in Reid, 1888: 468)

Referring to his experience of 'working men', Forster acknowledged some resistance to 'religion being pushed on them', but 'I am sure of this—the old English Bible is still a sacred thing in their hearts ... No measure will be more unpopular than that which declares by Act of Parliament that the Bible shall be excluded from the school' (in Reid, 1888: 489f.). While some MPs thought this was a move too far, for others it was not far enough: 'The idea of being suffered to teach religion, instead of its being made an integral part of every child's education! ... No education can impart moral principle which is worth the having in time of temptation except a religious one' (Colonel Beresford: Hansard 1870, CC: 222). The MP for Merthyr Tydvil, H. Richard, argued that compulsory religious teaching and worship in Prussia had produced an indifference to Christianity and that while an unchristian population was bad enough, an anti-Christian one would be worse (ibid.: 274). This was in the Welsh context of his arguing for religious teaching and observance to be left to the home, the chapel and denominational schools. Dr L. Playfair, the MP for the Universities of Edinburgh and St Andrews, argued that for many the Bible was the only means of culture and contained within it ennobling sentiments for children and profound poetry, along with the 'beautiful morality' of the New Testament. It was the task of education to offer 'invigorating stimulus, refreshment, hope, development', using 'the higher subjects' as well as the three Rs (ibid., CCII: 554, 566). This was similar to Matthew Arnold's views (see p. 38).

Francis Cowper-Temple, Liberal MP for South Hampshire, argued that the spirit of the Act was that of 'tolerance and comprehensiveness' and its provision could bring together 'the Churchman, the Dissenter and the Secularist' (ibid., CXCIX: 438). This vein of inclusivity was to remain an educational objective in the domain of spiritual development and religious education. Cowper-Temple argued that the state ought to be unsectarian but should be Christian. He is still remembered in RE as the architect of the 'Cowper-Temple clause'. Non-denominational schools should provide Religious Instruction: the Bible should be read and explained, and the Ten Commandments and the Lord's Prayer taught. To read the Bible without explanation, as some argued in an effort to avoid denominational division, would be 'unfair and cruel' to children. But in 1902 one MP was still recommending the reverent reading of the Bible on its own, with no commentary or explanation whatsoever, in board schools (Hansard 1902, CVII: 1159). Gladstone stated that the legislation was 'in a spirit of studied respect for religion' (Hansard 1870, CC: 298). But no one had quite addressed Oxford MP Vernon Harcourt's comment near the beginning of the debate, about curriculum control (ibid.: 222): 'It is unworthy of an English Parliament to send this great and important question of religious education [including spiritual development] to be dealt with by Town Councils and Parish Vestries'. More than a century and various landmark education acts later, the position was unchanged for RE. It was to be preserved as a local affair alongside but outside a national curriculum.

Much continuing political dabbling in values education was motivated by fear of a rising generation who might not know right from wrong, but Midwinter (1995) overstates the socialising intention of the religious provision. Perhaps values were being emphasised as education in beliefs was perceived as contentious. Sir Charles Dilke, MP for Chelsea, asked whether 'one religion [denomination] was to be picked out and made supreme, or were all religions to be taught?' (Hansard 1890, CC: 290). This was another issue that, transposed from Christian denominations to world religions, was still in hot contention after the 1988 Education Reform Act and Department for Education (DfE) Circular 1/94. The 'Cowper-Temple clause' in the Act illustrated the government's determination to avoid religious controversy by banning denominational teaching outside denominational schools (see also Copley, 1997: 40, 206). In 1870, in the climate of rivalry between powerful and influential denominations and the urgent concern to extend elementary education, it is easy to see how 'the spiritual' was not at the centre of thinking or legislation, but neither was it absent. Some of the seeds of later development are present in the debate and the legislation. But as the opposition to the Act by the Birmingham League and others continued afterwards, notions of the spiritual were overlaid by ongoing controversy.

The 1902 Education Act and provision for the spiritual

Although A.J. Balfour introduced the bill by describing the English educational system as antiquated and ineffectual compared to those of the USA, Germany and France, its main component parts were concerned with establishing local authorities for education;

dealing with higher education including teacher training; addressing elementary education; and a section embracing education committees, expenses, borrowing, schedules and a miscellany of matters. Despite impassioned opposition by the nonconformist lobby against 'Rome on the rates', rate aid was given to church schools, many of which were in dire financial straits, but their independence was curtailed as local authorities were allowed to appoint one-third of managers, HM Inspectors were allowed access and teachers' salaries were to be paid from the public purse. There was outcry about the cost to the rate-payer of supporting the voluntary sector, which then accounted for approximately 70 per cent of the nation's schools, containing half the school population. It was to lead to 38,000 summonses and 80 imprisonments for refusal to pay rates and ongoing acrimony that led to the defeat of Augustine Birrell's 1906 Liberal Education Bill and the abandonment or defeat of later plans for reform of the dual system. The 1902 Act addressed the system rather than the content of education. To go further might have reaped such intensity of vehemence, depth of controversy and the exercise of powerful influence as to thwart new legislation altogether.

Religious Instruction was dealt with, but in the context of the rightful use of monies by local authorities:

> 4.—(1) A council, in the application of money under this Part of this Act, shall not require that any particular form of religious instruction or worship or any religious catechism or formulary which is distinctive of any particular denomination shall or shall not be taught, used, or practised in any school, college or hostel aided but not provided by the council, and no pupil shall, on the ground of religious belief, be excluded ...

A.J. Balfour recognised the difficulties: 'We do not insist ... upon teaching the children of this country a particular religion. We do insist upon teaching them a recognised arithmetic, a recognised geography, history and so forth ... We are not agreed about religious education' (Hansard 1902, CV: 855). The requirements of 1870 about the timing of 'religious worship' and 'any lesson on a religious subject' were also retained, as was the clause preventing children being required to attend or refrain from attending a place of worship or Sunday school as a condition of membership of the day school.

But in severing the provision for worship in board schools from that of any denomination, a problem was created that was to haunt education for decades to come, namely that in the absence of denominational worship all that seemed possible was a lowest common denominator, i.e. a hymn, a Bible reading and a brief prayer. Lord Hugh Cecil, MP for Greenwich, sensed some of this:

> A board school is a school with only one door; the child goes in, learns a great deal that is valuable, and goes out again into the street. A Church school, a Wesleyan school, or a Roman Catholic school are schools with two doors, and the other door leads to the Church or Chapel ... Now what is it you want to do in regard to children? ... What is desired is *a religious habit of mind and religious customs*. (Hansard 1902, CVII: 848, my italics)

Another speaker, J. Bryce (MP for Aberdeen South), expressed a similar view, noting that parents did not care one atom about dogma. Cecil went on to argue that behind the denominational question lay the much more significant one posed by 'the real enemy, indifferentism' citing the statistic that only 6 per cent of Londoners were said to attend church. There was a clear awareness that if denominational teaching and worship could not be given in a board school, undenominational teaching and worship was far from problem-free. Griffith Boscawen (MP for Tonbridge) noted that the government seemed to think that religion could be taught which had no particular form. What was that religion, he asked. It was apparently '*some sort of religion of which the majority of people approved* ... It might be Mahommedanism [*sic*] plus Catholicism or Buddhism plus the Baptist religion ... It was perfectly clear that no such religion could exist' (Hansard 1902, CVIII: 551, my italics). Facing an amendment from A.E. Humphrys-Owen (Montgomeryshire) calling for board schools to open and close with religious worship, Balfour responded by asking what religious worship he had in mind. Balfour felt it might end up as anything which 'the fancy of the education authority might suggest'. He did not advise 'the impossible task of laying down the foundation of a universal Parliamentary theology' (Hansard 1902, CVIII: 361, 363, 367). Balfour recognised the problem, but did not solve it. Indeed, it is a commentary on the insights of this debate into the nature of the UK problem that by the end of the twentieth century, the matter

64

had still not been resolved, but the speakers' insights still applied, except by then it appeared that a universal parliamentary and DfEE spirituality had replaced what Balfour had called theology. Detached from the spiritualities of the churches and of the other religions, it was in similar difficulties to those anticipated in 1902 for non-denominational religious teaching. The attention given in the debate to the problems of single school areas, in which there was no parental choice between a denominational or board school, was an acknowledgement of another difficulty: that one's child might be placed in a school where the religious teaching and observance were not in accord with the parent's wishes. Only the withdrawal clause remained as an option here.

The 1917 Education Bill and the 1918 Education Act

The education bill of 1917, like that of 1944, was born in a climate of war, the desire for reconstruction and a greater willingness to countenance change. The issues it had to address included the extension of free secondary education, the employment of children, the school leaving age and 'continuation' education for the youngest people in paid employment. War meant that the nation had become more used to firmer centralised direction of its affairs. The Board of Education had recently adopted a suggestion to help to counter child neglect and abuse: that local authorities and voluntary bodies should establish play centres for children. This stemmed from ideas of Mrs Humphry Ward (see pp. 40ff). In Birmingham alone, 4,000 summonses for child neglect had been issued in 1917. Herbert Fisher left the Vice Chancellorship of Sheffield University to take up appointment as President of the Board of Education via election to the Commons of an uncontested seat at Sheffield Hallam. He sat as a non-party MP, enjoying the support of Lloyd George and A.J. Balfour.

Speaking in the House, Fisher felt that the war had at least created a better atmosphere on the bitter denominational question. F.D. Acland argued that it would be good to avoid religious controversy and that employers would favour an education system which produced a broader outlook and a keener intelligence than one aimed at greater specialisation (Hansard 1917, XCVII: 824). M. Barlow wanted to see 'a National Mission ... on education, to make the country realise what is involved in the future of the race, in seeing the education of the next generation ... put on a higher, better and more effective, but also ... a more moral and spiritual plane than it has ever attained in the past' (ibid., 1962). These lofty sentiments did not affect the legislative outcome for the place of the spiritual in curriculum terms in the 1917 bill or the 1918 Act. But Barlow's words were a distant echo of Thomas Arnold. Arnold wanted the church to rise above denominationalism; Barlow wanted education to rise above the damaging quarrels wrought by denominationalism. It was also one of the early appearances of the word spiritual in the discourse about education, meaning something much wider and more fundamental than merely the religious instruction slot on the timetable. The English began to perceive 'religion' as divisive and had plenty of evidence in the failed educational bills and thwarted plans of this period and earlier. 'Spiritual' began to be seen as something higher than denominational. Despite Fisher's careful negotiation with the churches and other interested parties, the bill was withdrawn by the government through lack of business time to steer it through Parliament. But substantially the same bill was re-introduced and passed the following year.

The 1944 Education Act and provision for the spiritual

Aspects of the preceding debate

The wartime climate of the 1944 Act, the negotiations with the churches about the denominational question and the future of the dual system, Butler's appointment to the Board of Education and Winston Churchill's idiosyncratic response both to educational change and to the place of religion in the system, have been addressed elsewhere (Chadwick, 1997: 25–39; Copley, 1997: 15–29). In this Act the term religious education was held to embrace religious instruction (the classroom subject) and worship (the whole school act of worship). Both RI and worship were almost universal in practice before the Act in both denominational and board schools, but the Act was to make them compulsory. It was not agreed without debate which concentrated on the problem of compulsion set against the notion of pupil entitlement and the implicit awareness that the removal of all religious elements in school life would simply produce a secular indoctrination: 'What I am anxious to ensure is that every child shall have the opportunity of daily collective worship provided and I think that schools should be compelled to provide that opportunity' (Godfrey

Nicholson, MP for Farnham, Hansard 1943, 397: 2396); '[Worship involves] the creation of an atmosphere pervading the life of the school and giving the school community a recognised character' (R.D. Denman, Leeds Central, ibid., 398: 1882). Not all the commentators were sanguine about the benefits: 'The act of worship is an interior thing which cannot be enforced by an external authority ... No Parliament and no authority can compel it' (Edmund Harvey, Combined Universities MP, who went on to compare Nebuchadnezzar's attempts to impose his style of worship in the Book of Daniel, ibid.: 2396). Lieutenant-Commander Gurney Braithwaite (Holderness), whose military title did not match his famous Quaker family names and background, spoke anecdotally about his childhood at a Quaker school, where he felt that compulsory worship produced an effect opposite to that intended: 'There was an element of ridicule, which developed rapidly among the scholars, at the number of times they were compelled to attend' (ibid.: 2399).

Various MPs were troubled by the application of compulsion. W.G. Cove (Aberavon) claimed that the repercussions and reactions might not be what MPs desired them to be, indeed that behind this process the Tories were using religion as a sanction for a reactionary social policy. E. Harvey (Combined English Universities) argued that once compulsory worship is enacted by Parliament, something has been done against the interests of religion itself (ibid.: 2414). T.E.N. Driberg (Malden) as an Anglican churchwarden was uneasy about compulsion. It reminded him of the 'Reich Christians' in Nazi Germany. Richard Acland (Barnstaple), a linear descendant of F.D. Acland (above, p. 65), whose colourful opposition to private education and strong support for equal pay for women teachers featured elsewhere in the debate, opposed compulsion (for Acland on RE see Copley, 1997: 18, 71–5). In a society dominated by 'money grabbing' and 'obsession with property', he wanted pupils to be 'constructive rebels'. He wondered why the government wanted to compel an arrangement that was 99.5 per cent present already in practice:

They are wondering whether in 20 years' time they will not be in need of this compulsion, feeling that the 99.5 per cent may by then have become only 90 per cent or 75 per cent. We are at a crisis point in the affairs of the world and the truths of Christianity have to be interpreted to keep abreast of the times.

> I get a little afraid when I see people asking for compulsory
> powers which can be used as a substitute for keeping the
> practice running. (ibid.: 2414)

N.A. Colegrove (the Wrekin) reminded MPs of the withdrawal
clause. It was not the case in his view that the state was compelling
worship. That could only be true if there were no withdrawal
rights. The legislation reflected 'a universal belief that the
education of this country must be built on a firmer spiritual basis'.

Professor W.J. Gruffydd (University of Wales MP) addressed the
issue of atheist headteachers leading acts of worship: 'A worse
thing than having an atheist headmaster conducting a service is to
have a headmaster whom the children can, by no stretch of the
imagination, associate with anything spiritual. It would be a
tragedy for a child to have his early life contorted and distorted by
such conditions' (ibid.: 2401). Gruffydd went on to argue that
religious observances in school are not a form of superior
education, nor are they to be done for ethical or moral reasons,
nor are they better when led by clergy; for 'the only priest and
celebrant should be the person himself, guided by the inner light
of conscience'. This was an early affirmation of the possibility that
spirituality could be quite separate from religious belief and that
it was at least in part an inner process which the ritual assembly
might or might not stimulate. It was a more secular version of the
Reformed Protestant view of the responsibilities of believers for
their own spiritual discipline, part of the doctrine of 'the
priesthood of all believers'.

Sir Harold Webbe (Westminster Abbey) wanted to revive 'the
spiritual and personal values in our society and in our national
life'. He urged that people 'have never been more ready for
spiritual guidance and leadership than they are today', while at the
same time accepting that a person's religion, creed and relationship
with their God is 'an intimate and personal thing'. It is the state's
task to see that the 'religious consciousness' latent in every child
is awakened and strengthened. It will provide the child with the
courage to adventure and the strength to achieve. The war has led
to new values. Past denominational divisions are now seen as
matters of detail not principle. A proper emphasis on the spiritual
in education will lead to a high sense of honour; a sincere love of
truth; a simple reverence in the face of those phenomena that
cannot be explained; and a readiness to put the service of others

above self-interest (ibid.: 1857). This is an early taxonomy for spiritual development (see p. 12).

But between Butler and Churchill himself appeared the seeds of the two strands of spirituality which were to dominate later debate. 'Rab' Butler, a practising Anglican who for thirty-six years was churchwarden in a rural parish context, was attached to the simplicity of quiet village services and was to find Christian consolation in the aftermath of the death of his first wife. As an undergraduate he had attended the lectures of James Frazer. Butler also had a Free Church pedigree through his maternal grandfather, George Adam Smith, theologian and onetime Moderator of the Church of Scotland. Butler admired William Temple as 'spiritually a first class athlete' (ibid.: 102) and the two found common ground. Rab's understanding of spirituality was based on Christian spirituality, which he saw as not so much something to force on children as an influence and treasure to which they should be introduced. Churchill, an agnostic with pantheist tendencies, wanted 'to introduce a note of patriotism into the schools' (Butler, 1971: 90) and to downplay direct references in the Act to religion (ibid.: 114). Churchill seems to have implicitly viewed spiritual development as a mixture of citizenship, pride in community and country, and a sort of muscular aestheticism. In 1944 the views of Butler were more typical of those who held educational office; by 1994 a modified version of Churchill's composite and only implicit view seemed to have become dominant. In 1998 David Blunkett, the New Labour Education Secretary of State, began to re-emphasise the role of citizenship as an expression of values in education to occupy up to 5 per cent of curriculum time. There was less talk of the spiritual.

The 1988 Education Reform Act and provision for the spiritual

Aspects of the preceding debate

The 1988 Act was born in a quite different context from that of the 1944 Act: peacetime, single-party government, the end of consensual politics, monetarist policies, 'Thatcherism' and a vastly more secularised and plural Britain. Kenneth Baker was the Secretary of State for Education who framed what became the Education Reform Act (1988). He saw it as unlike the 1944 Act, which was 'essentially a religious settlement ... I did not have to frame my Education Bill with the powers and responsibilities of the churches and other faiths at the forefront' (Baker, 1993: 207). This was an implicit acknowledgement of a secular agenda to be borne out in the lowly place of RE and worship in draft legislation. Baker was concerned that certain aspects of the 1944 Act, such as RE and daily worship, had 'in many schools fallen by the wayside or been transformed into other studies'. He wanted merely to enforce the 1944 provision for RE and worship. But he seemed naively unaware that by changing the entire curriculum map he had also changed the position of worship and RE: they were now isolated outside the new national curriculum. It was like putting a new skyscraper building beside an ancient church and claiming that nothing had changed for the church. Chadwick (1997: 90) argues that the National Curriculum proposals were 'dominated by a secularist viewpoint, indicative of an increasingly utilitarian and materialistic approach to education in which market economics would become the overriding ethos of schools'. All the government wanted was 'an historical development of the existing [1944] settlement' (Baroness Hooper, government opening speech on the Second Reading in the Lords, Hansard, 1988, 495: 1212).

A steady stream of written and oral questions in the Commons and the Lords, long before the education reform bill debates, had drawn attention to concerns by MPs and their constituents that the 1944 requirement was not being implemented for RI and worship. The government response is best summed up in the phrase 'complacent dissatisfaction'. Government answers revealed that the Department of Education and Science (DES) had no information about provision or withdrawals from RI and worship at local level, hence no national picture. They relied on parental complaints, which were few in number and in any case included cranks. Local syllabuses were given as the reason for no attempt at national provision in the reform bill, despite the expressed wishes of the churches. Angela Rumbold as Junior Education Minister in the Commons repeatedly emphasised the government's intention to strengthen the complaints procedure. This was scarcely 'reform' as suggested by the bill's title. The Prime Minister herself (Margaret Thatcher) answered a question in the House about the dangers of the 'trend to multi-faith education' and a call by the questioner to re-affirm the government's commitment to Christianity in the legislation. Thatcher stated rather incoherently that in the 1944 Act the central concerns of RI and worship were presumed to be predominantly 'the scriptures of the Bible [*sic*] and [some of us] are somewhat concerned that that [the 1944 Act] has not altogether been carried out' (Hansard 1988, 132: 501). Baroness Gloria Hooper for the government in the Lords, answering Lord Orr-Ewing (Hansard 1988, 492: 1187), said that schools should be sensitive to their multi-faith populations, that Christianity was still the dominant religion in many areas, and that proposals that worship should be 'in the main Christian' were related not to a percentage of the total acts of worship in a school but to the area in which the school was situated, something that was lost sight of in later debate. She added that schools should devise worship in which 'as many pupils as possible can participate'.

Baker encountered an unexpected reaction to his plans for RE and worship when the bill went to the House of Lords. A group of Conservative peers nicknamed 'the Tribe' by Bishop Graham Leonard, the Anglican spokesperson for education in the House of Lords, saw a chance to re-assert the Christian base of RE and collective worship by amending the bill in such a way as to make the position of Christianity within the legislation more explicit and more directive. They included Emily Blatch, John Boyd-Carpenter, Caroline Cox, Alec Douglas-Home, Rodney Elton, David Renton and Peter Thorneycroft. Their effect on the debate is detailed in Copley (1997: 135–46). It was clear from earlier questions and remarks that there would be troubles ahead. Baroness Jean Strange (Conservative) had already urged that school worship must include hymns. She quoted in full the first verse of 'All people that on earth do dwell' as a fine exemplar for children. She did not mention its doleful tune, or the problems of conscience that non-Christians called upon to sing it might experience. Hooper replied that such matters must be left to headteachers (ibid.: 1189). Viscount David Eccles (Conservative) accepted that a non-Christian could teach RE, but did not accept their credentials for leading worship. Lord Ritchie was quick to ask where in the proposals what he called 'the moral development bit' came in the list of subjects. He might have asked the same of the spiritual.

The Tribe's proposals for collective worship

On 12 May 1988, late in the evening, at the Committee stage of the bill, Lord Thorneycroft put forward his amendment (No. 222) which was to change 'collective worship' in the bill to 'collective Christian worship'. He pushed this to the vote at 12.15 a.m. and the amendment was carried 17–0. This caused the sitting to be suspended under Standing Order 15 as fewer than thirty members had voted. Baroness Cox re-introduced No. 222 on 16 May, arguing that school worship had become a secularised, politicised or multi-faith celebration of shared values. Cox was to emerge as a key player in the Lords debate.

She was puzzled that the amendment was not being backed by the churches. It should have been written in the 1944 Act: 'All we are trying to do is to ensure that our children have the opportunity to become familiar with the Christian language of our country.' (Hansard 1988, 497: 13). The Bible, hymns and prayers constitute spiritual resources and can provide help in times of need in adult life if they are familiar. Cox, herself a practising Anglican, had been awarded a peerage by Thatcher for her heroic resistance to left-wing tyranny at the Polytechnic of North London described in her co-authored book, *The Rape of Reason*. Cox explained in that book that in a professional situation little short of persecution, she had been personally sustained by the weekly eucharist, the words of her favourite biblical text (Joshua 1.9) and the ancient hymn 'Patrick's breastplate'. Like Thatcher she was a conviction politician, but unlike Thatcher she was not always pro-Tory. She had marched with the nurses' unions to support better conditions for nurses. In education, however, she steered a right-wing course. She cited T.S. Eliot's remark that a nation does not cease to become Christian until it has become something else. Viscount Tonypandy (George Thomas, a cross bench peer) supported her, stressing that 'the heritage of our faith must be passed to our children'. In the end the amendment was withdrawn. Thorneycroft felt that omitting the word 'Christian' would continue to allow what went on in school to degrade Christian worship, while writing it in risked a high number of withdrawals. Leonard set to work on a compromise.

The Lords Third Reading debate on worship

Two hours into the Third Reading there was a fifty-minute debate on school worship (see also Copley, 1997: 144ff.). Leonard proposed a five-point framework for worship which would 'maintain the tradition of worship as part of the process of education'; maintain the contribution of the collective act of worship to the establishment of values within the school community; not impose inappropriate forms of worship on certain groups of pupils; not break the school up into communities based on the various faiths of the parents; and be realisable and workable in practical terms of school accommodation and organisation. Leonard brokered what became the accepted final settlement by a skilful mixture of diplomacy and ambiguity. When he proposed that worship 'should in the main reflect the broad traditions of Christian belief in ways appropriate to the age, aptitude and family background of those involved', Thorneycroft pressed again for more explicitly Christian worship. Baker, who greatly resented the Lords and the Church of England tampering with his minimalist proposals for RE and worship, later remarked acidly: 'I can see why bishops move diagonally' (Baker, 1995: interview), although his memoirs record in a more conciliatory tone that Leonard 'struck the right balance' (Baker, 1993: 209).

The Lords and spiritual development

Although RE and worship were the central thrust of 'the Tribe's' concern, there were allusions at points in the debates to spiritual development. Lord St John of Fawsley, a former junior education minister and a leading Roman Catholic lay person, argued that spiritual or religious experience could have come to the UK by any number of means, via the Enlightenment, the *philosophes* in France, or through Hinduism, Islam or Buddhism. As a matter of historical fact it here came through Christianity. The adage 'no bishop, no king' has its modern parallel in 'no religion, no morality'. History affords no example of a society which has maintained morality without a religious base. Worship is not about forcing a form of commitment on young people but rather 'to open their eyes to the possibility of making *spiritual commitment*' (my italics). Our society is both multi-faith and Christian, Christian in the sense of possessing deep ethical instincts and in that 'we wish Christianity well' even though only a minority are churchgoing Christians (Hansard 1988, 498: 18, 650). To be effective, spiritual development should be undertaken in a broadly Christian context. Our society might have chosen a secular, agnostic model; in fact it has never shown any inclination towards this.

Lord Max Beloff (Conservative) stated that from a Jewish point of view giving prominence to Christianity implied that other religions were second class. Lord Donald Soper (Labour), a veteran Methodist cleric and peer, pointed out that 'Christianity' embraces a variety of attitudes, some preferable to others (ibid.:

20). But for Cox it was fundamentally about entitlement: 'Many of our young people have been denied a spiritual vision and we have allowed too many of them ... to grow up without knowledge of the faith of their forefathers ... [a] betrayal of their spiritual heritage' (ibid.: 643). Cox's biographer (Boyd, 1998: 421ff.) presents the issue as the Children of Light (Cox and the Christian lobby) versus the Children of Darkness (educational professionals including many RE teachers and left-wing dogmatists in league with prevaricating Anglican bishops in the Lords: 'her most vociferous opponents were from the multi-faith lobby', ibid.: 423). This is simplistic. But his analysis exposes *en passant* the disappointing failure of the Tribe to engage in real dialogue with the education professionals about the art of the possible. Instead the Tribe turned to religious leaders who favoured separatism in worship and RE, often on the grounds that this protected the purity or integrity of each faith. If the Lords had a view of spiritual development, they never considered it to be value-neutral. Lord Immanuel Jacobovits, the Chief Rabbi, identified the 'real enemy' not as heresy or apostasy but 'paganism', reflected in rampant and pernicious moral anarchy. By paganism he did not appear to mean those religious groups which describe themselves as pagan, or the 'old religion', but secular unbelief. He quoted Proverbs 22.6: 'Train up children in the right way and when they are adult they will not depart from it.' Not all peers agreed. Lord William Sefton of Garston (Labour) rejoined that it was not paganism that had persecuted witches. He was also cautious about the word spiritual, 'which can mean anything ... The teaching of morality could be expressed as spirituality' (Hansard 1988, 496: 428). Leonard retorted that 'the religious dimension of life does not make us human. It enables us to be fully human' (ibid.: 433).

Here we have all the terminological problems of the debate about spirituality also present among education professionals alongside the lack of definition. Is spiritual synonymous with religious or Christian? Is it a more aesthetic version of moral? Undermining the intentions of the Lords lie the same ambiguities reflected in professional writings before and after the Act.

The Legislation

1 (2) The curriculum for a maintained school satisfies the requirements of this section if it is balanced and broadly based

curriculum which—
(a) promotes the spiritual, moral, cultural, mental and physical development of pupils at the school and of society ...
6.—(1) ... All pupils in attendance at a maintained school shall on each school day take part in an act of collective worship.
(2) The arrangements ... may, in respect of each school day, provide for a single act of worship for all pupils or for separate acts of worship for pupils in different age groups or in different school groups.

6 (3) required the arrangements for worship in country schools to be made by headteachers in consultation with governing bodies and in voluntary schools by governing bodies in consultation with headteachers. (4) required that worship be conducted on school premises with (5) special occasion exceptions for aided, grant-maintained and special agreement schools.

7.—(1) ... In the case of a county school the collective worship required by section 6 of this Act shall be wholly or mainly of a broadly Christian nature.
(2) For the purposes of subsection (1) above, collective worship is of a broadly Christian character if it reflects the broad traditions of Christian belief without being distinctive of any particular Christian denomination.
(3) Every act of collective worship ... need not comply with subsection (1) above provided that, taking any school term as a whole, most such acts which do take place in school do comply with that subsection.

7 (4) allowed within (1) and (3) schools to take into account (5) circumstances relating to the family backgrounds of the pupils, their ages and aptitudes and (6) that a Standing Advisory Council on Religious Education might determine that (1) might not apply to a school or a class within a school and that worship of schools receiving such a determination must not be distinctive of any particular denomination but might be distinctive of a particular faith.

9 (3) If the parent of any pupil ... at any maintained school requests that he may be wholly or partly excused ... from attendance at religious worship in the school ... the pupil shall be so excused accordingly until the request is withdrawn.

11 (1) defined the role of the Standing Advisory Council on RE (SACRE) in relation to collective worship as 'to advise the authority (i.e. the local education authority, LEA) on such matters connected with religious worship in county schools ... as the authority may refer to the council or as the council may see fit'. 12(1) awarded it the power to dispense with the requirement for Christian collective worship for a whole school or a class within it in the case of an application by the head of a county school after consultation with the governing body. Such a 'determination' is subject to review after not longer than five years has elapsed (12 (6)). Sections 84 to 86 dealt with worship in the new grant-maintained schools and required it to conform to their previous foundation tradition, as county or voluntary aided or voluntary controlled schools.

Commentary on the Education Reform Act (1988)

Nothing more was said about spiritual development. A number of possibilities account for this. One is that it was held to be subsumed within RE (as a curriculum subject) and daily collective worship. In that case 'spiritual development' would replace what the 1944 Act understood by Religious Education, which was held to comprise Religious Instruction (the classroom subject) and daily worship. Another possibility is that spiritual development was intended to permeate the whole curriculum as a cross-curricular theme. In that case one has to ask how. If it is present everywhere, how is this distinguishable from its being nowhere? The other possibility is that the provision was token and that the phrase was used with no particular meaning except to signal that education was not to be seen in entirely materialistic or vocational terms and that the spiritual was not being entirely forgotten in a market economy. At the time the anxiety of headteachers was much more directed towards the tightening of collective worship and, for some heads, the provision elsewhere in the Act for grant-maintained status for schools choosing to opt out of LEA control. RE teachers were more concerned to explore the curious 'basic subject' status allocated to their subject. The spiritual was, once again, overlooked.

Hull (1990: 63f.) tried to make sense of the provision for worship. It could not legally be 'Christian worship pure and simple'. It had to 'reflect', not even possess, a broadly Christian character. It had to be 'mainly' not 'wholly' broadly Christian. It had to reflect the traditions of belief, not worship, i.e. it was not expected to copy the worship of the churches. The participants never lose their status as pupils or students; they are never treated as believers in a gathered faith community. But Hull noted that this was within a context that still takes a Christian norm (strictly a broadly Christian norm) for county schools. The cultural context of this, however, that the UK could still be said to be a 'broadly Christian' but by no means a Christian country, was less discussed (though see Copley, 1997: 2–8, 187f.; Davie, 1994: *passim*).

The broadly Christian base line for school worship was to pose a major problem for other faith communities, notably Islamic ones. Halstead and Khan-Cheema note that one set of figures suggests that there are now two practising Muslims in Britain to every five practising Anglicans (in Francis and Thatcher (eds), 1990: 199) and that the gap is closing. They had no equivalent concept of breadth: 'broadly Islamic' was held to be meaningless. 'Islam, as Muslims never tire of repeating, is a unity and complete way of life' (ibid.: 202). They also could interpret the Act as a piece of Christian imperialism. For Muslims any scheme of worship must treat Islam and other world religions with justice and with equal respect, must avoid Christian indoctrination, must not take place from a secular viewpoint and must not be neglected in schools as a low priority (ibid.: 202f.). Circular 1/94 was to exacerbate the situation further. Equally it posed a problem to humanist groups who were supportive of assemblies 'to affirm and celebrate the worth-ship of the shared values of the school community' (British Humanist Association, 1991: 1), but were opposed to assemblies for worship of a deity.

As the 1990s advanced, Christian views divided further over the issue (Chadwick, 1997: 104f.). Some held that worship should now be voluntary; some held that it should be less frequent than daily; others argued for the legal *status quo*. All recognised the need for sensitivity, not merely towards other religions, but to the personal response of all pupils. Efforts were made to convince MPs that schools were trying to carry out the spirit of the law, if not Circular 1/94, rather than the daily letter.

The 1992 Education Act and provision for inspection

The 1992 Schools Act reiterated the importance of the spiritual, moral, social and cultural development of all pupils and required these areas to be inspected by Ofsted. The 1995 revision of the

Framework for Inspection emphasised that inspection in these fields should concentrate on, the extent to which a school was providing its pupils with 'knowledge and insight into values and beliefs' and enabling them 'to reflect on their experiences in a way which develops their spiritual awareness and self knowledge'. It is interesting to note the language here: into the field of 'spiritual development' appears a different category, 'spiritual awareness'. Chadwick as a headteacher herself noted confusion in the whole area of spiritual, moral, social and cultural development: if inspections reported an orderly atmosphere did it mean that schools were good morally? Was social compliance evidence of moral development or an ethical framework? Was there a danger in trying to structure the spiritual dimension? Could children be 'spiritually developed' without any knowledge of God? (Chadwick, 1997: 112). Perhaps the cynical interpretation of what teachers called 'SMSC' was valid (see p. 9). Certainly the tendency among religions to produce 'rebels' and nonconformists as prophetic figures did not appear in concepts of 'SMSC'; such tendencies in pupils might not be appreciated in a 'SMSC' rating.

Perhaps the confusion over 'spiritual' was more than semantic and philosophical. During a time when the Conservative governments took less and less notice of the churches, the mainstream churches were seen less and less as partners, more like sectarian interest groups, despite their still holding 20 per cent of the nation's schools. Thatcher, as a 'conviction' politician, had taken little notice of anyone, as she believed that vested interests would dilute or subvert her proposals, professions being seen as a conspiracy against the 'non-expert', reflecting the victory of the producer over the consumer. In such a free-market situation, spiritual development is hard to identify in a plural society whose *de facto* moral values appeared to be the survival of the fittest.

After the 1997 general election the effort by New Labour to create a feel-safe situation for the electorate led to a continuation of Conservative commitments in the economy and no major change in education, symbolised by their leaving in post Chris Woodhead, the Chief Inspector of Schools, a very controversial figure among practising teachers, and his re-appointment without advertisement of the job in 1998.

DfE Circular 1/94

Circular 1/94 was probably written by Baroness Emily Blatch, a member of the 'Tribe' (see p. 71 and Copley, 1997: 177). Legally, like all such Circulars, it had the status of guidance. It opens with an expression of concern that 'insufficient attention has been paid explicitly to the spiritual, moral and cultural aspects of pupils' development' (1/94: 9, 1). A note of 'deep concern' is added that RE and daily collective worship are not being provided 'with the frequency required or to the standard the pupils deserve' (ibid.: 9, 5). The aims of collective worship are defined:

> to provide the opportunity for pupils to worship God, to consider spiritual and moral issues and to explore their own beliefs; to encourage participation and response, whether through active involvement in the preparation of worship or through listening to and joining in the worship offered; and to develop community spirit, promote a common ethos and shared values, and reinforce positive attitudes. (ibid.: 20, 50)

It went on later:

> 'Worship' is not defined in the legislation and ... should be taken to have its natural and ordinary meaning. That is, it must in some sense reflect something special or separate from ordinary school activities and it should be concerned with reverence or veneration paid to a divine being or power. ..[It] will necessarily be of a different character from worship amongst a group with beliefs in common. The legislation reflects this difference in referring to 'collective worship' rather than 'corporate worship'. Collective worship and assembly are distinct activities. Although they may take place in the same gathering, the difference between the two should be clear. (ibid.: 21, 57f)

The explicit 'advice' that worship was directed to God may have seemed self-evident to the Junior Education Minister and her advisers. Parents objecting could avail themselves of the withdrawal clause and remove their children from collective worship. This was the tired old Tory response to provision for RE and worship that kept insisting that by tightening the complaints procedure all problems would be solved. But in the schools the situation was different. Headteachers had been using collective worship as integrative community assemblies to affirm common values, in practice usually moral rather than spiritual. Such assemblies at their worst could be dull, spiritless affairs, with heavy moral homilies by the headteacher or other leading members of the school establishment, but in an apparently secular society they were supported, or at least not actively opposed, by parents including humanists and others whose life stance was secular. Some secondary heads were also angered by the statement: '"Taking part" in collective worship implies more than simply passive attendance... [It] should be capable of eliciting a response from pupils, even though on a particular occasion some of the pupils may not feel able actively to identify with the act of worship' (ibid.: 21, 59). In some secondary schools the collapse of compulsory hymn singing and the moral difficulties of compulsory spoken prayers had led to passive audiences, whose engagement if any was cerebral. The Circular seemed to be tightening a situation which heads already found constricting. Worse was to come. The Circular went on to discuss the position of 'some non-Christian elements' in collective worship content. Some would not deprive it of its broadly Christian character, nor would elements common to Christianity and another religion or religions. But 'It must, however, contain some elements which relate specifically to the traditions of Christian belief and which accord a special status to Jesus Christ' (ibid.: 21, 63).

The secular assembly was no substitute for what Circular 1/94 proposed. Of course, Muslims accord a special status to Jesus but as prophet, not Christ, and this was clearly not what the Circular had in view. Circular 1/94 also countenanced different religion assemblies for children formally withdrawn from collective worship (ibid.: 25, 88). It seemed as if the Junior Minister was willing to pay a price of different religion assemblies in order to preserve, if necessary, what was assumed to be the majority 'broadly Christian base'. Yet the Circular wanted 'children who do not come from Christian families' to 'be able to join in the daily act of collective worship' (ibid.: 65). Perhaps these children were those of no religious background. The additional Circular advice that headteachers should now keep plans and records of collective worship (ibid.: 22, 67) was wise. Controversy might lie ahead and documentation would be important if a formal complaint were made, or if Ofsted wanted evidence about the nature of collective worship over a term as a whole.

But many heads and teachers did not feel themselves to be even 'broadly Christian'. Nor did they wish to be involved in the mental gymnastics of devising acts of worship that were more Christian than had recently been the case, but yet in which children not from Christian families could join, and all against the background of no professional training themselves in the field. Their professional associations rose in anger against 1/94, although it was not always remembered that legally this was advice, not statute. The National Association of Headteachers asked how schools could ensure active involvement if most of their pupils were Muslim (Bulletin, February 1994). The Association of Teachers and Lecturers asked why Circulars were being used to promulgate the personal predilections of ministers (*Times Educational Supplement*, 4 February 1994). The General Secretary of another union, the National Association of Schoolmasters/Union of Women Teachers (NASUWT) protested that 'Ramming Christianity down all pupils' throats will not change society's values which have been so undermined by the sleaze and commercialization associated with this Government' (in Chadwick, 1997: 98). It could have been Richard Acland speaking in the 1943 Commons education debate all over again (see Copley, 1997: 71f.).

Professor John Hull analysed the implicit theology that lay behind this: Christianity has to be seen as distinct from 'other religions', pure in integrity, powerful in predominance, extending separation and competition into the place of worship (Hull, 1993). The Churches Joint Education Policy Committee argued that the Circular definition of worship should be broader. Members of the Evangelical Alliance, who might have been expected to press for the retention of the 'daily' requirement as a form of mission, were in fact divided on the matter. At the same time there was a less publicised feeling among some who might not support the Circular, but felt that headteachers had not really faced up to implementing the existing law on worship and that many people 'are more at ease with their sexuality than their spirituality. Certainly schools have become less inclined to address moral and spiritual truths, let alone assert them' (*Times Educational Supplement* leader in Chadwick, 1997: 98f.). But opposition to the Circular and in particular to the 'daily' requirement of the Act continued to grow, rather than diminish. In 1998 the National Association of Headteachers reiterated its position that the daily requirement was impracticable; that the 'broadly Christian' requirement was 'dogmatic and insensitive', that heads were supportive of assemblies to address 'spiritual, moral and ethical issues in the context of the school's values and activities'; and that they wanted flexibility. They asserted that people can be moral (they did not claim spiritual) 'without coming from a particular religious base generally, or from any particular religion' (in the *Church Times*, 12 June 1998).

Circular 1/94 was a massive 'own goal' by the government and the DfEE, unless one argues for a conspiracy against RE and related activities within the DfEE (see Copley, 1997: 130). It strengthened the opposition within the teaching profession to any inclusion of worship (an activity that none of them had been trained or in any way prepared to conduct) and to a lesser extent increased the case against the spiritual dimension in education by many different interest groups, not all of whom were conscious of the secular implication of their own agenda. It paved the way for Michael Barber, head of the Standards and Effectiveness Unit at the DfEE, to argue that citizenship should replace religious values in education (speech to Secondary Headteachers' Association 1998), and a QCA report on citizenship (1998) in which the spiritual is prominent by its absence. The case for secularising education was strengthened by the ineptness of Circular 1/94, but yet the death of Diana, Princess of Wales in 1997 (see p. 2) demonstrated that in Britain the death of God, or at least of spiritual feelings and aspirations that were certainly far from secular, had been greatly exaggerated. Her death challenged the climate of individualistic hedonism; it provided a shocking and public reminder of mortality, that even the young can die. Even without conspiracy theories about the car crash in the Paris tunnel, it made dark forces seem real. The tragic incompleteness of Diana's own search for a spiritual position perhaps spoke to the condition of many. In her funeral address her brother, the Earl Spencer, affirmed the need for her boys to 'experience as many different aspects of life as possible to arm them *spiritually and emotionally* for the years ahead' (in the *Observer*, 7 September 1997, my italics). If Circular 1/94 was an attempt by a minority to inflict Christianity on a reluctant education profession, secular abolitionists themselves constituted merely another minority with an agenda of their own. But they continue to be the undoubted beneficiaries of it.

Chapter Three

Curriculum Development in the Domain of the Spiritual

The 'Christian era' of understanding spiritual development

Underhill (1927: 177) was clear that the child has a spiritual faculty, the roots of which lie in the feelings rather than the intellect and that education should involve developing the bodily, mental and spiritual faculties of the child. She was clear that the universal tendency of life and of religions is to point to God and that so often the dogmas that agnostics reject are theological caricatures of the truth. She indicated the implication for curriculum: 'The religious exercises [in schools], whatever they are, should be in common, in order to develop the mass consciousness of the school and weld it into a real group' (ibid.: 198). For her the appeal of the heroic in history lessons was a pointer towards the spiritual life. The people treated as heroes are of 'the fullest vitality and immense natural attraction'. Nature and aesthetics, including poetry, are also curriculum stimuli towards the spiritual. For Underhill God is transcendent, yet is also the indwelling spirit of love, beauty and power. Her period bridges the Victorian and the post Second World War situation. Some of the Victorian emphasis on Christian values in education remains, but it is recognised that other factors—welding the school as a community, developing children as individuals, identifying spirituality as a cross-curricular theme—are important. These factors were gradually to assume more importance, while the Christian value base was to recede, first the doctrine, then the ethic. Sandhurst faced his young school leavers with the question whether humankind is a highly developed animal, or has a spiritual mind or soul (Sandhurst, 1948: 22). He included aesthetics, sub-divided into Beauty, Goodness and Truth, in his short course for army cadets (ibid.: 105ff.). He linked spiritual development with leadership and citizenship and queried whether a person can have any notion of citizenship if they 'think that they are mere animals without purpose or supernatural destiny'.

By 1966 education was recognisably more secular in its values. Hilliard was then Reader in Education in the University of London, having taught in schools at Snaresbrook and Ely and worked in higher education in Sierra Leone and Ghana. He could point to a secular definition for religion in an unnamed influential American philosophy of education text, as 'the spirit in which one holds one's supreme value—the value in terms of which one values all else' (in Hilliard *et al.*, 1966: 14). He cites as philosophical leaders in this secularising tradition H.G. Wells, Julian Huxley, Bertrand Russell and H.J. Blackham. But it was not peculiar to the UK and included the 'Death of God' theologies in the USA. Hilliard saw this as a sharp and fundamental divergence from Christianity, the reduction of educational aims to those of secular personal development. He finds evidence of it in major education reports in which Christianity, if present at all, is present as a confused undercurrent: Crowther (1959), Robbins (1963) and Newsom (1964). This had not always been the case and Hilliard briefly reviews history from early Christian times. Early Christianity did not exhibit such conformity to 'pagan learning' but from the sixteenth century onwards humanism ran alongside Christianity in the education system and Christian thinkers failed to integrate it into their philosophy for education; eventually it almost overcame Christianity to triumph as secular humanism. Hilliard argued that a new 'Christian humanism' was called for. It did not happen. Instead the secular tide advanced, accommodating *en passant* the increasing pluralism in UK society, or at least in UK cities. The secular world view displaced religion either into the category of minority hobby, the sanitised version of religion, or publicised the dangerous psychotic tendencies of rampant fundamentalism, the unexpurgated version.

School worship 1944–1968

The classic exposition of worship within the context of the 1944 Act's intention, but in a society which seemed to be becoming less Christian, was by Hilliard (1963:160ff.). He was also writing in a context of growing iconoclasm in RE (Copley, 1997: Chapter 3 *passim*). Hilliard argued that Religious Education, which in the 1944 legislation embraced classroom RI and whole school worship, was 'more than teaching about religion in the classroom: it is also the provision of the opportunity for the child to enter into that fuller religious experience which is to be found in worship'. Hilliard recognised that the climate of teacher opinion was abandoning this view and retorted by quoting William Temple: 'While it is objectionable to force the teachers to conduct prayers against their consciences, it is also objectionable to force the children to omit prayers for the sake of the teachers' consciences' (in Hilliard, 1963: 168). While a valid reply philosophically, it also indicated *en passant* that the problem had been noted more than twenty years previously, when Temple wrote. Worship was thus to Temple and Hilliard an entitlement for young people, which without provision in school they might never receive. Hilliard's views were swept away, first in the 'anti-confessional' approach to RE of the 1970s, which discredited Christian approaches to RE and education in general, and then in the tide of secularism which rendered all religion peripheral in the mind of the majority as the decades advanced.

In the wake of the 1944 Act advice was given in agreed syllabuses about worship. Cambridgeshire saw it as an influence that sets the tone for the day, in which the teacher's demeanour is a crucial factor. It requires an orderly entrance and exit by pupils, planning well in advance, brief, intelligible readings and the appropriate use of silence (Cambridgeshire Education Committee, 1951: 12f.). The London syllabus saw worship as affirming all that is latent and best in school life, but it becomes 'unreality' when its concerns are divorced from those of the school (London County Council, 1947: 21f.). Worship is the response of the soul to that which it values supremely. It is good only when the object of worship is worthy; there was perhaps an echo here of the danger of alternative spiritualities within Nazism in the recent past. The key factors for successful school worship were identified as planning, brevity, reverence, avoidance of too much repetition (some was seen as helping to make fine biblical or other passages memorable), involvement of the pupils, 'the personality of its director', the avoidance of 'condescension, sentimentality and priggishness' and the provision of space and seating (ibid.: 22). The Cheshire syllabus too affirmed the importance of worship in the life of the school and the need for good planning (Cheshire County Council, 1951). These could not alter the increasingly crowded accommodation in some schools, which meant that the act of worship for the entire school meant that the pupils had to stand throughout the occasion. If they were also clad in outerwear such as anoraks, ready to move across a campus to Period One, it helped to create an atmosphere of transitoriness, that the act of worship was really a minor ritual prelude to the real business of the day, lessons. It was a waiting room. In such a situation quality, however defined, would be hard to attain.

The comment in an Institute of Christian Education Report of 1954 that children need educating in how to use worship and what to do was to go largely unheeded for the next fifty years (Institute of Christian Education, 1954: 90); it was perhaps the only area of a school's activity into which children were never explicitly inducted or allowed to question. The London Agreed Syllabus of 1947 had foreseen this (London County Council, 1947: 25). The Oxford Handbook recognised the growing difficulty of compulsory worship in a secular society and quoted Bonhoeffer on religionless Christianity (City of Oxford, 1963: 38). It considered that school worship was 'precariously poised'. More conservatively, Cornwall was defending the centrality of the Lord's Prayer, but warning against sermonising and the use of old-fashioned missionary hymns (Cornwall County Council, 1964: 14, 16). For the West Riding (West Riding County Council, 1966: 118) planning, reverence and participation were the keys. Lancashire could propose worship as the 'feeling' aspect of RE (the classroom subject was seen as the intellectual side) but it also identified the right atmosphere as crucial (Lancashire Education Committee, 1968: 13). Defence of the old assumptions varied, perhaps according to the religious composition of the local area and the strength of alternative secular life stances such as humanism, but there was a universal recognition of problems.

One perennial problem of school worship at all times was its 'voracious appetite' for material (Brandling, 1989: xx). 'Assemblies, like television, are great devourers of talent' (Egan, in General Synod Board of Education, 1983, Introduction). Publishers could guarantee steady sales of anthologies of improving literature for use in assemblies over many years. They are in many ways the stale successors of the Victorian improving books for children which Lewis Carroll (1832–98) and E. Nesbit

(1858–1924) had so successfully undermined. Study of the contents of assembly anthologies over decades is a window into the preoccupations of those leading the occasions. Prescott (1953), for instance, includes a section on the 'faith of the heroes'. Nineteen heroes, all male, are selected, and in further prose extracts a passage from Queen Elizabeth II's 21st birthday radio broadcast is the only one by a female. In a sequel (1955) two out of fifteen heroes are female, Elizabeth Tudor and Christina Rossetti. The paradigms are of Christian example, self-sacrifice, courage in the face of odds, service of others, missionary endeavour in the face of adversity and the willingness to lose material comfort in order to retain what was later called the moral high ground. Grace Darling (1815–42), who rowed out with her lighthouse-keeper father to help to rescue survivors of *The Forfarshire*, and Gladys Aylward (1902–70), who spent her entire savings on a single ticket to China to go out as a missionary in 1930, later leading over a hundred children on a mountain trek to safety from Japanese invaders in 1938, are two recurring female exemplars. Mother Theresa was to follow in later decades. Like Gladys Aylward, another regular post-war assembly figure from the pre-1944 era was Lawrence Oates (1880–1912), who, impeded by severe frostbite, deliberately sacrificed his life on Robert Scott's South Pole expedition by walking out of his tent into a blizzard in order not to handicap his companions. He in turn had overtaken an earlier generation of Victorian heroes such as General Charlie 'Chinese' Gordon (1833–85), an idiosyncratic evangelical Christian officer who died defending Khartoum, abandoned by the inept British government response to the Mahdi's siege. Fearless English Christian men, ready to lay down their lives for King and Country, provided an interesting role model prior to the Great War. Gordon was particularly suitable: he was an avid Bible reader, worked tirelessly to help orphans, was devoted to the concept of doing one's duty, rediscovered what might have been the site of Calvary and, whichever detailed version of his death one accepted, died valiantly in an entirely hopeless situation (Pollock, 1993: 316ff.). These and other assembly role models offer a fertile field for further research: to identify and analyse the religious and moral qualities being promoted in such case studies, gender stereotyping and variation, and generational differences, and to include archive and empirical study into their continuing influence on the memory of those who heard about them in school.

May and Johnston (1968: 98ff.) offer a window into worship at the midway point between the 1944 and 1988 Acts. They see the act of worship as a vehicle for RE and a natural activity for Christian teachers to lead, but they are also aware of queries and doubts about its usefulness. In response to these queries they affirm the usefulness of assembly in promoting community, in training for civilised group behaviour, in relating to 'our own cultural tradition', and as an opportunity to allow children 'to glimpse something of what the religious vision is'. Their survey evidence revealed varying practice: some schools separating notices from the act of worship; some mixing 'ritual, reverence and friendly informality'; themes for the week; a committee taking responsibility rather than just the headteacher; a tendency in some schools to displace the headteacher as the authority and centre-piece of the ritual. A 1965 National Opinion Poll survey is quoted by May and Johnston (1968: 117) in which 84 per cent of parents stated that school worship was an important part of the life of state schools and 88 per cent wanted provision to be continued, even if no longer on a compulsory basis. In answer to another question, 18.9 per cent opposed the compulsory provision of worship.

School worship 1969–1988

Accommodating the multi-faith situation
Cole (1983) recognised that until about 1950 the only religion represented in schools in significant numbers was Christianity, but that this was emphatically no longer the case and that non-worship assemblies that affirmed the values of the school community might be the way forward in an increasingly problematic situation. He did not want the school to lose opportunities to express its corporateness. Different religion assemblies, with the consent of the school, was another option, as were voluntary and separate religion acts of worship. Cole argued for the values assembly option, but in which each culture and faith might contribute its own insights. The aims of these assemblies would be to awaken aesthetic awareness; to reflect on experience, awareness of human issues and possible responses; to explore what it means that the school is a community; and to examine all this in a wider way than is possible in the classroom (Cole, 1983: 193). Hymns, the Lord's Prayer, even theistic but not specifically Christian songs (participative music as worship would be unacceptable to Islam),

would all have to disappear. But readings from the scripture of a religion, with a period of reflection or a prayer which pupils were asked to reflect on but not pray, would have place. Visiting imams, rabbis, vicars etc. would have to be trained to be sensitive to the multi-religious situation. Cole saw assembly as 'a rich activity in which diversity and unity are openly celebrated, accepted and explored'. He saw problems in schools which had a mainly white staff and mainly 'non-white' pupils where the law might be seen to force the Christian religion onto the pupils.

The Fourth R (1970, see also Copley, 1997: 97f.) was a thorough and reasoned enquiry into RE chaired by Ian Ramsey, Bishop of Durham. It was far-sighted and perceptive but it never received the government attention it deserved, perhaps because it was too easy for the Department of Education to dismiss it as a church-sponsored document. Although Anglican in provenance, it had consulted widely in the course of its work and had received evidence from teacher associations, and secular bodies such as the British Humanist Association and the National Secular Society. It therefore offers a wide window into attitudes towards worship at the time. The Headmasters' Association supported 'Morning Assembly' as a 'vital and real experience in the daily life of the school' (*Fourth R*: 306), whereas the Headmistresses' Association saw a case for replacing 'daily' with 'regular' (ibid.: 313). The Assistant Masters' Association preferred less frequent worship, perhaps twice weekly (ibid.: 317), while the Assistant Mistresses' Association could only note divergent views but agree that big schools had more problems with worship (ibid.: 319). The County Councils' Association saw merit in some acts of worship in smaller units than whole school and argued that a complete secularisation of public education would deny a basic part of each child's nature, the spiritual (ibid.: 337). The British Humanist Association wanted worship to become an optional extra-curricular activity after school (ibid.: 327). In one sense the report looked backwards in its own views: RE would be 'inadequate and unbalanced' if separated from worship; RE without worship is 'like geography without field studies' (ibid.: 60f.). In other ways it was very honest, noting a range of opinions from the ecclesiastical to the secularist and 'no lack of horror stories' on worship as it really was in schools and divided opinion on whether daily worship was desirable (ibid.: 130f.).

It identified the case for school worship (ibid.: 131f.): worship offered an experience of worship for RE purposes; public opinion supported it; rituals meet deep human needs; staff and pupils who are Christians can dedicate themselves and their work to God while others can reaffirm their personal ideals and values; there is a loosely defined but observable tradition of worship in English life (Christmas, Easter, Remembrance Day etc.); it expresses the corporate life of the school and its removal could simply promote secularism. The case against was seen as the Christian pre-suppositions of school worship; that real worship is an interior state and cannot be compelled; that school worship disallows discussion and questioning, laying itself open to the charge of indoctrination; that some humanist teachers feel hypocritical in engaging in it; and that school accommodation is sometimes not conducive to holding acts of worship. Many independent schools were fortunate to have chapels, which enhance the atmosphere for worship, but they had big problems themselves with compulsory worship (ibid.: 161f.). The report admitted 'grave social problems' in growing multi-ethnic areas; and that worship is often so badly done as to be counter-productive. *The Fourth R* did not see regular inter-faith worship as a solution to some of these difficulties (ibid.: 141) but it did commend careful experimentation where there was common ground between faiths present in a school. It was extremely sensitive in its examination of the issues, but the report did not identify many solutions to the problems surrounding worship, other than properly to indicate that abolition was not the easy and value-free solution it might superficially appear.

By the mid-1970s the situation had shifted further. Moreover, it was developing against the backcloth of a quest in classroom RE for 'neutrality' on the part of teachers (Copley, 1997: 100ff., 107ff.), which had the effect of isolating worship further as a defensible educational activity. These were years of RE teachers distancing themselves from leading worship as public acolytes of the headteacher and of the burden passing to year heads in the growing comprehensive schools. Year heads were emerging in such schools in a middle-management pastoral and administrative role and they were seen as the *de facto* heads by children in their year group, to whom the headteacher might be a distant figure in a school of 1,000 or more pupils. Acts of worship often became year group events and not whole-school events, unlike those in the tripartite predecessors of comprehensive schools in which the headteacher could lead a whole school act of worship assembled in the hall. But heads of year received no training to lead acts of worship and again it was assumed that on promotion to that post the right skills would somehow emerge.

Even in this inhospitable climate, worship had some defenders. Attfield (1974: 172ff.) argued that only assemblies for worship which addressed God constituted a problem. He identified the case for worship as a necessary activity to understand religion, but he conceded that observing the worship of believers could suffice just as well for this purpose. He argued that to choose whether to worship or not, one has to be taught how to do it. He noted the problem with this was whether worship can precede religious commitment and raised the question whether agnostics could be encouraged to pray on an 'as if' basis. Cole (1974: 11) saw worship as 'declamatory', unlike education which was exploratory. Worship did not allow for freedom of response. Jean Holm could ask not only whether teachers *should* be providing worship, but whether they *could*, in the non-faith context of the county school (Holm, 1975: 120). She proposed to revert to assemblies which would explore awe and wonder with younger children and questions of meaning with older ones. But they would no longer pose as worship. Webster (1974: 55ff.) opposed the view by some that the presence of non-believers at acts of worship would be beneficial to them. He noted that in some situations major religions banned them (e.g. in the Jerusalem Temple, beyond the Court of the Gentiles, and in Mecca). Schools should instead, he argued, provide opportunities for members of their communities to practise their ultimate commitments.

Tompkins (1976) was part of the mid-1970s swing away from worship. She argued for assemblies as potential providers of a variety of teaching and learning situations based on the individual's need to relate to larger groups and applying Phenix's realms of meaning: symbolics, empirics, esthetics (*sic*), synnoetics, ethics and synoptics. Holley (1979: 68f.) suggested that worship might have a part to play in Religious Education, in nurturing human beings and the socialisation of children in terms of a particular view of humankind.

Hull (1975) notes a consistency in understanding of the nature of school worship from about 1939 to the mid-1970s. Despite changes in methods used in worship, he argues that the concept itself had altered remarkably little and that this was broadly the same as that held by the churches. He could have added that for more than a century school worship had been recognised as a problem, of denominational conflict, or of pupil response, and that over this period it had become detached from curriculum and that the emerging views of spiritual development were emerging without reference to worship as a central activity. In a later piece Hull defines worship as the response to that which is of ultimate concern, drawing on Tillich (Hull, 1984: 12), arguing that school worship does not bite sufficiently deeply into the matters of ultimate concern to pupils. 'Our task in school assembly then is to take the most transparent, the most symbolic, of the concerns of our pupils, in the hope that they will be led from the trivial and immediate and the local to the significant, the enduring, and the universal concern' (ibid.: 13). But Hull was equally clear that achieving this would not constitute an 'act of worship'. For Hull, the attempt at 'worship' was preventing an educational potential which the assembly might otherwise realise: ultimate concern and joyful affirmation in a 'frankly secular setting'.

Copley (1989) later described the underlying basis for worship in the non-church school as a sort of residual and largely secularised non-denominational Protestantism, ritually represented by the gowned secondary school head conducting an abridged Free Church act of worship: hymn, reading, exposition, prayer, dismissal. It presupposed an essentially passive congregation in an almost entirely auditory context and could be said to have declined in popularity in parallel with Free Church worship. In primary schools there was more pupil participation, but secondary school worship had a tradition of difficulty that could be traced back to before the war, both conceptual and practical. Its presupposed Christian base had reduced or disappeared. Members of other religions were now present in many schools, as were children who were conscious of themselves as agnostics or atheists. In addition, the idea of communal hymn-singing (or singing at all) and praying had acquired the sort of odour of conformity about it that adolescents were keen to dissociate themselves from. There was passive non-cooperation in many secondary schools after the first year or two. The only immediate effects of trying to address the difficulties were to render the pupils even more passive: many schools abandoned hymns and the attempt to force pupils to say the words of prayers, and provided instead a reading and a homily, usually of a moral rather than a religious or spiritual nature.

The final contribution to the pre-1988 debate about worship was made by Watson (1987). She argued that the 'wholly educational' case for worship had hardly been given a hearing: true worship encourages an open not a closed mind; education has underestimated the religious commitments of school students; participation in worship is educationally necessary in order to find out what it is about, i.e. to make a reasoned choice; school worship can be an affective part of RE; it can alert pupils to secular conditioning. But it must not attempt to compel belief or participation such as saying Amen after prayer. It is reminiscent of the view evinced by Randolph Crump Miller (in Durka and Smith, 1979: 107–20), that Whitehead's dictum that religion is a response to a vision of something requires a corollary, that worship is a response to the vision, an exploration of the visceral and emotional, rather than the mental and intellectual. It affects the right lobe of learning. Miller was, however, writing in the US context in which worship was not a feature of school life, but only of the life of faith communities.

School worship 1988 onwards

The effects of the Education Reform Act (1988) on school worship had more immediate impact on secondary schools than primary. The relaxing of the requirement that the whole school should assemble for worship and at the start of the day meant that many headteachers were suddenly in danger of compliance with the law. They could no longer use as an excuse for non-provision of daily worship for all pupils that they would not fit into the hall, which most comprehensive schools had long outgrown. Tutor group provision of worship was now legal and, from a timetable point of view, very easy to deliver. The problem was the form tutors. It was one thing for form tutors to sit with their forms passively in a year group or house group act of assembly, joining in with varying degrees from total attention to surreptitious marking of the register. It was quite another to be expected, with no training, to lead an act of worship in the form room with a group of twenty-five or thirty indifferent or hostile adolescents. Some form tutors signalled that in such circumstances they would exercise their legal right to withdraw. Others read from a sheet distributed by the head of year an adage or short passage based on the theme for the week. The danger was that this could easily become a Christmas cracker motto occasion. Everything depended on the tutor's commitment to the task and their relationship with the class. Rather than precipitate a crisis of mass withdrawal at tutor group level, which did occur in some schools, some headteachers continued not to implement the daily requirement for all pupils in their school. But even then they remained unhappy that they were being forced into a corner which threatened either their integrity or their legality in compliance with statute.

Faced with these anxieties and the possibility of a charade for pupils, a comprehensive school deputy head argued for a new model for secondary worship based on the Radio 4 *Today* programme's *Thought for the Day* (Copley, 1989). In this peak-time daily radio slot, at about 7.50 a.m., a member of a faith community or a humanist offered from their tradition a 'thought', designed to provoke or stimulate their hearers, without in any sense attempting to proselytise them. At the time the most successful exponent of this on the radio was Reform Rabbi Lionel Blue. His mass audience found his thoughts uplifting or helpful or entertaining. They did not convert to Judaism, nor was that ever the intention of the broadcast. In the adaptation for schools it was not intended that the audience should be passive, or that the 'thought' should be entirely auditory as on the radio programme. But it offered a context for worship which could be honest and allowed the pupil freedom of response. They were asked to listen to the thought and reflect on it, not to express ritual or credal agreement with it. An examination of the role of silence in collective worship followed (Copley, 1992), in which it was noted that silence allows pupil freedom; is non-divisive; and contrasts with the busy-ness of daily life. But it was noted that the use of silence in school worship owed more to its potential educational value than to any silent religious tradition and that even the Religious Society of Friends (Quakers) had not found the use of silence to be problem-free.

Despite the pressure in the Act and in Circular 1/94 to take worship seriously, no money was provided by government for training, research or in-service training of teachers in leading collective worship. A small sponsored research project, the Worship in Secondary School Project (WISSP) based at the University of Exeter School of Education in collaboration with the trustees of Westhill College, Birmingham, itself raised the monies to finance a video filmed in schools in the West Midlands and the west country (Copley, 1994). The DFE refused to finance it. One training video was a drop in the ocean of what was to be needed if teachers were to be empowered to conduct collective worship well and to be inducted into the debate about what was and was not possible. But the inspection of schools after the Act did lead to more discussion and thought being put into collective worship at school level than had perhaps been the case for decades. It also led to more vigorous forward planning and to record keeping, in case schools were challenged by inspectors or complaining parents to show how they had fulfilled the 'broadly Christian' requirement, taking a term as a whole.

Watson (1993), examining structures for collective worship, argues for inspirational input such as music, a reading or something visual; space to reflect, including training in stillness; a specific religious component presented as an invitation to take religion seriously; a controversial element to remind everyone that consensus is neither assumed nor sought; and short sentences to remind people of the educational purpose of the assembly. Such occasions may not be worship so much as worship-enabling. For McCreery (1993) school worship could be a unifier, a celebration of shared values, a time for reflection, preparation for voluntary corporate worship outside the school and part of spiritual development.

The demands created by the new Act for collective worship materials were no less than those in the 1944 Act, and there was increased demand in schools which were now being required to increase their number of acts of worship to comply with the Act. The stream of anthologies continued unabated to meet these needs. There was a tendency away from individual exemplars towards themes. Blatchford (1992) has Being Human, Education, Faith and Religion, Global Village, Shakespeare's Universal Themes, Equal Opportunities, Science and Technology, Rights and Responsibilities, Heath and Environment, Justice and Ideals, and the Media. His keynote pupil responses are: awareness, appreciation, respect, preference, commitment, devotion, adoration. Self (1996) includes a section on 'Saints are sinners who keep trying'. There is a shift in value judgements. For Peirce (1992: 1) 'it matters not so much which "religious" order one belongs to, but how we treat one another in this multi-racial society ... it is the well-rounded person that is important'. Clearly, beliefs and life-stance do not matter, in collective worship at least. Karin tells pupils that collective worship is about 'withdrawing for a moment from the din and distraction of our daily routine, to relax in the quiet of our hearts, and listen—listen to the awesome mystery at the centre of our personality. Religious people call this mystery God. Call it what you like ... ' (Karin, 1995: 2). Norton (1998) tries to include activities for children that do not revert to hymns and the Lord's Prayer, retaining 'Famous People', three out of nine being female. The *Primary Assembly File* (1995) offers regular mailings of new material to its subscribers to meet their quantitative needs. This was an interesting parallel to the mail order services supplying sermons, which for more than a century had helped some hard-pressed preachers to survive Sundays. The *Primary Assembly File* aims 'to provide a framework around which people with a religious faith or none can unite with honesty and integrity' (1995: 1). It was a long journey from 1944, although it is hard to see how collective worship could have survived at all as a universal school activity without some sort of metamorphosis along these lines. The real question was, what value did it have? Collective worship seemed to be trapped within a triangle of tension: the legal requirement; the need to protect the integrity of pupils and teachers involved; and the implicit requirement that the event, as a school-based activity, must have educational value. It is easy for individual acts of collective worship to attain any two points of this triangle of tension, but much harder to demonstrate that they can satisfy all three.

In a significant but neglected study, Webster (1995) took the view that school worship might invoke the spiritual by means of poetry, or great art, or story. The act of worship fosters the view that human beings are mysterious and unexplained (Webster, 1995: 94). All in the school community walk in a pilgrimage which throws up archetypal experiences: 'when they know they are in the labyrinth and come close to Hell's doors; when they make their own search for the grail; when they engage in the traditional rites of passage; when they are taxed with the delights and horrors of their own sexuality' (ibid.: 95). Collective worship stands within the spiritual dimension because 'it will not allow human beings to forget that their "existence is altogether in parenthesis" [D.Jones, *In Parenthesis*, Faber, 1937: p.xv] ... it illuminates the ways in which people relate to each other, as well as the care they show for each other, and the responsibilities they are prepared to shoulder ... it reminds men and women that knowledge and experience do not give them a home ... it interrogates those values which lie within the school community' (ibid.: 93–101). It makes clear that each of the disciplines of knowledge seems to rest on canons which are not derivable from, but which transcend, its subject matter.

Attempts to implement spiritual development and collective worship at LEA level: Case Study 1, Wandsworth (1990)

Wandsworth SACRE published a fourteen-page paper on this in the wake of the Act (1990). Like many of its type it outlined the legal arrangements but unlike most similar papers it entered into both a philosophical and pedagogical discussion of what implementing the arrangements might mean. It offered two general aims for collective worship: to give expression to the common values which underpin the school's existence as a community; and to provide experiences which strengthen attitudes and dispositions in all pupils so that those with a religious commitment may worship more adequately and the uncommitted may develop a capacity at least to approach the 'threshold' of worship (3.1). This retained the educational tradition of inclusiveness, which was defended expressly (ibid.: 3.4) against exclusive interpretations of the Act. Like learning in the curriculum, worship was seen as open and exploratory, something which should be offered in a way which was both educationally and theologically acceptable. The paper recognised that 'exploring "inner realities" is not easy' (ibid.: 3). To create a unique experience in worship it recommended that consideration be given to use of the following: song; reading; defined order and free expression; speech and silence; formal and informal seating; sitting down and standing up; eyes open and eyes closed; food and drink; prayer spoken or silent; meditation and contemplation; reflection (ibid.: 4). Two pages were devoted to interpreting worship and interpreting collective worship. Appendix 2 contained definitions of worship from Christianity (including Old and New Testament usage), Hinduism, Judaism, Islam, Sikhism and a Humanist understanding of worship as to do with worth and worthiness, recognising, affirming and celebrating certain realities and values. It contained 180 suggested themes for collective worship in Appendix 3.

A spider diagram attempted to reflect the dimensions of children's spiritual development which were identified as: symbols and rituals; beliefs and teachings; value and attitudes; ultimate questions; lifestyle and behaviour; and the Transcendent. The latter was footnoted as beyond the range or domain or grasp of human experience, in theology (of God) having existence outside the created world.

SCAA analysis of SACRE reports, 1997

Nearly all primary schools were reported as providing daily acts of collective worship for their pupils. In secondary schools, however, 80 per cent or more were said to be failing to comply with the daily requirement for all pupils. Where collective worship of good quality was observed, it was seen to contribute significantly to the spiritual, moral, social and cultural development of the pupils. Collective worship was noted as a feature of in-service training programmes in nearly all LEAs. It was a response to the Act and to inspection. Determinations listed from the normative arrangements were largest in Bradford (sixty-eight in total) but the figures were incomplete and unclear for many other LEAs. Twenty-four LEAs had provided no SACRE report at all.

Spiritual development 1988 onwards

New Methods in RE: An Experiential Approach, a formative text, was published in 1990 (Hammond *et al.*, 1990). It took the view that to understand how somebody else experiences the world, 'we have to take their inner experience seriously, and that involves an awareness that we have an inner experience of our own' (ibid.: 7). It reflected that religion is often seen as cold and unattractive, whereas spirituality makes people think of personal matters like prayer, meditation and love (ibid.: 9). It set itself to explore 'the personal experience, the inner *intention*' (ibid.:10, their italics). Such writing had a ready appeal not only in RE, which was reacting against the formal and exterior presentations of religion dominated by phenomenology arising from the Ninian Smart *zeitgeist* of the 1970s, but to those in search of a taxonomy to bring RE closer to Personal and Social Education (PSE) and spiritual development. The writers themselves had tried to avoid a secularisation of their work by indicating that there is no understanding of the religious believer without an awareness of the specific religious response experience to 'a sacred dimension to reality' (ibid.: 10), but they concede that the model of the person in PSE often seems to be drawn from a secular perspective and that it is highly suitable for their approach (ibid.: 17). It was an approach to spiritual development drawing on the writings of Bruno Bettelheim, James Fowler, Alister Hardy, David Hay, Anthony De Mello, Rudolf Otto, Edward Robinson, Evelyn Waugh and others. But it transformed classroom practice in RE in many schools (Copley, 1997: 165–9) and it was clear about the spiritual:

> The spiritual life, the life of wrestling towards enlightenment, and hopeful confidence in self and world, involves words, images, ikons, actions, chants, stories, koans, parables, music, candles, physical exercise, breathing and posture, mantras and mandalas, creeds and doctrines, silence. There are many techniques, many actions taught by the spiritual director ... (ibid.: 216).

It was a new gospel for RE and spiritual development. But it carried its own problems: in distilling a taxonomy of spirituality from different religions, had a hybrid been created which belonged to none of them, in which the process, not the destination, mattered more? Was not the teacher, whose awesome power to structure the inner search in the classroom, akin to spiritual director, but without the training, experience or wisdom? If, in the inner journey of pupils, demons come to the surface, who would exorcise them? Nevertheless, the 'new methods' moved RE away from 1970s and 1980s phenomenology allied to the pretence of neutrality in teaching. *New Methods* faced, even embraced, the subjective, providing a link with spiritual development at the same time.

Webster continued to provide commentary from a mystical-affirming position: 'Perhaps spiritual development is akin to the distinction between those who see that literature moves them to be total human beings, and those who read only with the blindness of physical sight' (1995: 108). Webster's view on the role of teachers in spiritual development is that they cannot climb the ladder for their pupils, but they may hold it and advise them how to climb. For him, spiritual development can occur within all the physical and psychological growth phases, even in the very young, but its necessary psychological precondition is symbolisation. The presence of more diverse contexts experienced by the growing child does not guarantee spiritual development, but such development is defined as 'that growth which, taking place in a multitude of contexts, slowly displaces the ego as the centre of all concerns and moves towards others in a thoughtful, caring and loving openness' (Webster, 1995: 111). Five key features of creativity will encourage it: a search for meaning; an openness to life; a union with the world; self-actualisation; and self-transcendence.

During a two-year secondment to the Anglican diocese of Salisbury as an advisory teacher, Beesley (1990) developed an approach through stilling, 'an activity which offers young people a variety of procedures and techniques for acknowledging, exploring and developing the spiritual dimension of their lives' (Beesley, 1990: 3). He sees it as a key by which pupils might become aware that they have an inner life, a dynamic, creative area which cannot be measured and dissected. By use of stilling and breathing exercises, then guided imagery and fantasy, his aims are to encourage quiet reflection; to improve concentration and self-control; to develop the ability to find inner peace; to promote awareness of the self's imaginative potential; to appreciate silence as a means of conversation; to understand how some of the deepest spiritual insights are accessed through stillness and silence; to enable pupils to cope with anxiety and stress; and to foster individual self-confidence and friendly relationships (ibid.: 5). This is not unique as an approach or a taxonomy. What made Beesley different was his ability to derive this explicitly from the Christian tradition. He did it, in a sense, as a servant of the church in education. A companion book took the method into tutor group collective worship, including teaching the skills for worship, something Beesley believed had been almost completely neglected. His view was that pupils cannot worship until they have been taught the skills. Beesley records positive pupil response to these methods. He was filmed at work with a class and in a subsequent interview with himself and Year 9 pupils by Copley (1994). Beesley interprets these spiritually oriented activities as open to Christian understanding: they can be glimpses of the Kingdom (ibid.: 49). For him the omission of the word 'God' in pupil comments and the secular appearance of the exercises is no evidence of pupil rejection or denial of the divine. He relates his work to biblical example: Elijah and the sound of silence; the Psalmist's 'Be still and know that I am God'; Jesus's experience in the desert etc. (ibid.: 51). He wants pupils to encounter 'the heritage of Christian mysticism ... not as something they merely read about in a book, but which is accessible to them in their own experience' (ibid.: 52). 'It may be that in being open to enjoy the goodness and stillness and awareness, students encounter the Godness of all things visible and invisible, and the Word in whom all things were made' (ibid.: 52). The drawbacks were that not all practitioners of this method would share the Christian spiritual base as their approach and that, while Beesley keeps the door open for a Christian response without attempting to compel one, an only slightly different way of handling the same techniques and occasions could close it.

Rodger wrote for a situation in which different religions and none would be the life-stances of pupils. He noted that spiritual development is *not* a subject, that it is *not* the preserve of RE, that it is not *knowing* something different, but a different *way of knowing* (in Best (ed.), 1996: 60ff., his italics). It entails a new quality of attention to experience in which we must silence and still 'our clamorous efforts to fit the whole of reality into our conceptual framework'. We have to rehabilitate teachers and pupils after the damage done by our culture to the capacity for spiritual awareness. Different techniques can help: parable; questioning; situations of dissonance; Zen Koans or jokes; empathetic listening; drama; role play; silence; meditation etc. Teachers should themselves be part of the process of spiritual seeking.

For Mott-Thornton, the approach embodies values and assumptions that can be labelled neo-romantic because they attempt 'to nourish a child's spirituality through focus on the natural and pure realm of his or her own experience, gathering self-evident values, uncontaminated by the wider society or any "theological" tradition ... This suggests an inherent individualism ... ' (in Best (ed.), 1996: 84). Watson (1993) pinpoints the weaknesses of the experiential approach in the *New Methods*: that it fails to make links with specific world religions; that while it purports to promote pupil freedom, it is within a structure imposed by teachers; that it appears to be abandoning the mind as a means of knowing and moving among unstated assumptions akin to Zen Buddhism; that it can be superficial and, badly practised, can confuse introspection with meditation; and that it requires a sophisticated level of participation to be successful. As a gateway to the spiritual she prefers Berger's five signals: the sense of order; the phenomenon of play; the experience of hope; the concept of damnation (cosmic injustice to be put right); and the fact of humour (Berger, 1970: 70ff.). For Berger these are 'prototypical human gestures', reiterated acts and experiences that appear to express essential aspects of human existence, but point beyond. They are not unconscious, like Jung's archetypes, but belong to ordinary, everyday awareness. For instance, the comic reflects the imprisonment of the human spirit in the world and by laughing at it, implies its temporality. Watson adds her own signals of transcendence: a sense of wonder at beauty; artistic creativity; the experience of personal rapport with others; altruism; the fact of love (Watson, 1993: 78). For Watson spirituality concerns a quality of life which transcends the natural plane and resists what might be called the unnatural, evil or demonic. Her view is that the 'seemingly flowery language' used in discourse about spiritual experience results from an inability to use religious language properly.

> All major religions offer a deepening understanding of spirituality because of the way they enable people to be consciously in the presence of that Mystery. True religion makes spiritual progress easier because it provides a vocabulary, a structure and a community, all of which can help people to attend to this dimension. Religion also provides many inspiring examples as well as yardsticks to chart progress and guard against the hijacking of high intentions by evil forces, however these are understood ... Talk of the spiritual can help revitalize religion. (Watson, 1993: 83)

Thus Watson sees the link between the religious and the spiritual as indissoluble, just as in worship she does not accept that attempts to give the word worship a general meaning (worth-ship) are other than an evasion of the problem. For Myers (1997: 76f.) examining the relevance of rituals in the everyday life of young children and the significance of these rituals for adults within the context of religious experience provides a way to discuss spirituality within the public arena. The possibility of using what she calls the 'S' words—soul, sacred, spiritual and sin—are then opened.

Webster too wishes to keep open more than secular solutions to the spiritual issue. Curricular response must spring from: the value set upon people; the Beyond and the approach to it; and the value of dialogue (in Best (ed.), 1996: 246). 'When all the myths are shredded and all of the slogans trumpeted, the only role the curriculum has is to enable youngsters to become human beings' (ibid.: 250). For Webster it is an ancient quest, at least as old as Socrates, who was critical that the Athenians gave so much time to acquiring money, honour and reputation and gave so little to thought to truth, understanding and the perfection of their souls (ibid.: 256). Spiritual development is the antidote for Webster to the instrumentalism and pragmatism that have rewritten the agenda for education.

Spiritual and Moral Development—A Discussion Paper *by the National Curriculum Council (1993)*

Aware of the problems and confusion surrounding 'spiritual and moral', as teachers then referred to it in shorthand, the National Curriculum Council published a discussion paper. By then 'spiritual and moral' were part of the inspection framework for schools and required comment when schools were under inspection. The paper identified component aspects of spiritual development: beliefs (personal beliefs including religious beliefs); an appreciation that people have individual and shared beliefs on which they base their lives; a developing understanding of how beliefs contribute to personal identity; a sense of awe, wonder and mystery, 'being inspired by the natural world, mystery or human achievement; experiencing feelings of transcendence, which may give rise to belief in the existence of a divine being, or the belief that one's inner resources provide the ability to rise above everyday experiences; search for meaning and purpose, reflecting on the origins and purpose of life and responding to challenging experiences of life such as beauty, suffering and death; self-knowledge, an awareness of oneself in terms of thoughts, feelings, emotions, responsibilities and experiences; relationships, recognising the worth of each individual, developing a sense of community, the ability to relate to others; creativity, expressing innermost thoughts and feelings through, for example, art, music, literature and crafts, exercising the imagination, inspiration, intuition and insight; feelings and emotions, being moved by beauty or kindness, hurt by injustice or aggression, a growing awareness of when it is important to control such feelings and how to use them as a source of growth' (National Curriculum Council, 1993: 2f.).

This represented a brave attempt to chart the territory for spiritual development in a way that would not prove offensive to religions, nor to those who rejected a theistic view of life. It linked spiritual development with curiosity and imagination, urged that deprived of such growth young people might be damaged in their social development and relationships with others and that such deprivation could leave them 'in an inner spiritual and cultural desert' (ibid.: 3). But the paper rejects the view that pupil progression in the field can be linear or that it could be assessed in individual pupils. Assessment could be intrusive or highly subjective (ibid.: 9). Ofsted was to inspect the provision and not performance, through discussions with the headteacher and staff, collective worship and lesson observation. The whole-school ethos, all curriculum subjects and collective worship were seen as agents for spiritual and moral development (ibid.: 6). It was extending this into practicalities which produced problems for the report: how can one change whole-school ethos? How is it produced? By whom? What does it mean that pupils should be 'encouraged to reflect on the possibility of certainty' (ibid.: 6)? In a relativist culture, the certainty of possibilities seems far more real. But the paper had clear value judgements in it: pupils should question 'the often exaggerated view of the infallibility of science as the only means of understanding the world, and the equally exaggerated view of the inadequacy of religion and philosophy' (ibid.: 6). Schools were encouraged to agree and promote 'core values' acceptable to all in the community. This was later extended to a national attempt to do the same by the School Curriculum and Assessment Authority, the successor to the NCC and then inherited by QCA, the successor to SCAA. Spiritual development was thus in the hands of unelected quangos, to be implemented by untrained headteachers and assessed by school inspectors whose other work was geared towards scoring performance and measuring progress. It did not quite correspond to any of the historic settings in which spirituality had blossomed or new prophets had arisen. The quangos had some specialist RE officers, but it is unclear to outsiders how far these officers in their quasi-civil servant role could shape policy or whether and to what extent they had effectively braked the worst excesses of political dogma in private.

Erriker (1998) points out that the quagmire of notions of spiritual development called for more radical action and that the options included: abandoning talk of spiritual development and replacing it by moral, working towards more rigorous definition, conducting research in the area, recognising the need to address how cross-curricular issues can be firmly identified in curriculum subjects, or using the opportunity to revise our understanding of the relationship between curriculum and education. What in fact followed was more of the same.

Attempts to implement spiritual development and collective worship at LEA level: Case Study 2, Solihull (1995)
Recognising that in large secondary schools, the daily requirement for collective worship often involved tutor group occasions for worship and that this was a task for which tutors were rarely trained and often ill-equipped to cope, a LEA RE inspector and three heads of RE departments working in Solihull schools produced a 332-page collection with two years' worth of photocopiable *Thoughts for the Day* for tutor group use. Among the aims for pupils are: to have a quiet moment during the day for reflection; to be able to explore their personal spirituality in a relevant way; to have the opportunity to extend their emotional repertoires; to explore themes from a variety of cultural perspectives. There is a theme for the week, linked explicitly to 'SMSC', and within it a theme for each day. It is envisaged that the tutor group will be standing as this 'sets an appropriate tone' (Solihull, 1995: vii) and that the event will last one or two minutes. Quality is held to be the key factor. Stimulus material can be read by or to pupils and the five questions included with each *Thought* can be used as the basis for group discussion, if time permits, or for reflective silence. A single 'Reflection/Prayer' is included with each piece and tutors are encouraged to see themselves as trustees of collective worship with their group, introducing it with a phrase such as: 'So to finish, a few words which you can make into a prayer or reflect upon for yourself'. The reflections are not often dependent on religious language. It is then recommended that the story/text can be affixed to the tutor group notice board at the end of the act of worship. The material represents the best tradition of teachers trying to implement difficult legislation in a plural and secular classroom world and to produce something on which staff and pupils could unite, rather than divide. It reflects the conviction of the writers that it could be done. Anecdotal evidence is included of the effect of this sort of collective worship

on pupils (ibid.: ix), although much more research could be done into this. Whether it can overcome the reluctance felt by many form tutors to handle this activity would depend on how far they were trained to lead it.

Education for Adult Life: The Spiritual and Moral Development of Young People, *a School Curriculum and Assessment Authority discussion paper (1996)*

The preamble to the SCAA discussion paper pointed out some of the problems: parental concern about the issue, coupled with lack of confidence; pressures on modern youth including advertising images and 'a synthetic youth culture' (1996: 5); the desirability of broadly agreed definitions for values, attitudes and morality; that spiritual and moral education are 'indispensable aspects of education for adult life ... [to] be promoted through all the subjects of the curriculum and through the ethos of the whole school..[that the issues] are not for education alone, but for all those involved in creating the society in which we want to live and work'(ibid.: 5). It was suggested that spirituality might mean 'the essence of being human, including the ability to surpass the boundaries of the physical and material'; development of the inner life, insight and vision; an inclination to believe in ideals and possibilities that transcend our experience of the world; a response to God, the 'other' or the 'ultimate'; a propensity to foster human attributes, such as love, faithfulness and goodness, that could not be classed as physical; the inner world of creativity and imagination; the quest for meaning in life, for truth and ultimate values; the sense of identity and self-worth which enables us to value others (ibid.: 6). Spirituality is seen as a powerful force, which determines what we are, our outlook on life and the world, and consequently shapes our behaviour. It can be the source of the will to act morally. Spiritual development may need help, like fostering a talent in music (ibid.: 6). Spirituality might be developed by means of religion, thinking, prayer, meditation or ritual, through awe and wonder, through positive relationships, even through negative experiences such as pain. The essential factor in cultivating spirituality is reflection and learning from one's experiences. Spiritual development should challenge scientism, make values in curriculum explicit, and have an impact when curriculum deals with ultimate questions such as creation. School worship was commended for its potential to allow quiet reflection and stimulating input of a type not necessarily encountered elsewhere in the school day.

Erriker (1998: 59) argues that the SCAA understanding of spirituality, embracing a broad range of views on the nature of spirituality and the means of fostering spiritual development, is directed to a moral end, proposed to be arrived at by consensus. Consensus, according to Erriker, is precisely the relativism attacked by Nick Tate, the Chief Executive of SCAA. Erriker proposes to replace it by a proper understanding of relativism, not as an 'anything goes' position, but one in which different 'spiritual voices' must be heard from faith and non-faith positions, without allowing any position to construct the foundations of the consequent development. Erriker reaffirms the importance of listening to children's narratives as the foundation for understanding their spirituality and helping them to schematise from these. This reverses provision based on creeds, whether secular or religious, or provision based on consensus among adults, and acknowledges in the growing child the possibilities of responsible citizenship. Erriker sees this as spirituality before morality, children's understanding before adult instruction.

It is a confused and plural picture that surrounds spiritual development at the end of these various legislative and curriculum processes. The Christian base has gone, or at least lost control in this area. Although Beesley, Watson, Webster and others have suggested a reconstructed base for understanding spiritual development which allows for religion, it has not caught on. Erriker and others have suggested a child-centred way forward, but as in so many child-centred programmes, it is dependent on a view of childhood supplied by adults and is therefore more complicated than at first appears. Quango documents in their efforts at consensus have gone for common denominators, which have in turn led inevitably into a secular cul-de-sac. No one can describe the curriculum position of 'spiritual development' as strong as the new millennium approaches, nor does what is happening or being proposed for schools readily relate to or reflect popular spirituality such as that so suddenly exposed at the death of Princess Diana.

Chapter Four

Some of the Ideas Roots for 'Spiritual Development'

Methodology problems

In undertaking to attempt to trace the development of the concept of 'spiritual development' in the English and Welsh education system, there is a serious methodological difficulty in that there is no clear historical and philosophical route that can trace the idea from a fixed genesis into the current situation. The term 'spiritual development' is recent and, to one commentator at least, inimical (Thatcher, 1991: 23). It is a complex conglomerate which has evolved rather than been shaped by individuals. At times it has appeared a hydra, multi-headed and evasive. Yet even such conglomerates have antecedents. They are rarely entirely novel. But over the last 150 years there is no common language in this particular discourse and no obvious linear path by which one can reconstruct 'development'. 'Development' in this context is at least as problematic a term as 'spiritual'. Only 'human development' is a less contentious phrase, but that is only because its usage is primarily biological and secondarily psychological. Human development can be related to stages of life, puberty, menopause, Piagetian levels of thinking etc. Moreover, it must be asked whether current notions of spiritual 'development' are a regression to a pre-Great War set of assumptions (see p. 48f), which ignore the capacity of humankind for what religions call sin.

There is inevitable discontinuity in the route that follows. Some of the people cited would not have been aware that they had contributed to any discourse on spiritual development in education. Some would have had no particular interest in the field, or in education itself. Other names are missing. For where moods, as opposed to systems, arise in philosophy or religion, exhaustive study of their sources is impossible. Thus we can speak only of 'some of' the ideas roots for spiritual development. The chapter could easily be expanded to become a book in its own right and still not survey the full field. Yet each strand or thinker selected made a discernible contribution to the complex of meanings that spiritual development had acquired by the end of the twentieth century. The phrase 'ideas roots' has been preferred in the chapter title to 'philosophical roots', as it has already been noted that the ideas which influenced spiritual development came from a much wider base than that of philosophy. The contribution of philosophers is indisputable. But there is a penumbra of influence which embraces literature, poetry and popular culture as well as philosophy. Snyder (1968) argues that spiritualities are rooted in communities and that communities themselves are made up of people from other times and places as well as those who live in them in the present. We meet the deceased members of communities through the memories of others, but also through their writings, art, music and stories, and we take some of their experience into ourselves. These are the keys, for Snyder, that enable us to develop spiritually.

The difficulties are not such as to invalidate the attempt. Despite them there are some discernible historical links in the tradition of spiritual development (see pp. 32–44), through the Arnold dynasty and their marriages, through the Arnold cult among later headteachers, and by a different sort of family tree from Rugby School alumni including the Temples, father and son, and personal encounters between leading figures in the story such as William Temple and Rudolf Otto. At other times it seems that the British roots of spiritual development can be traced back to Coleridge (who deeply influenced Thomas Arnold), though as in so much else Coleridge was at once incisive, seminal, scattered and unclear on the spiritual. Kierkegaard appears here as an exception, precisely because he has been largely ignored in the education debate on spirituality, rather than because of any quantifiable influence. On what grounds can he be excluded? It seems that he does not fit in. Kierkegaard was in so many a ways a misfit that this is his challenge to systems in religion. His caustic view of spirit challenges the current comfortable one. He is the Eeyore of spiritual development. At the end of the chapter an attempt will be made to synthesise the cultural shifts identified and the contribution made by the thinkers selected.

The Protestant principle in UK education

Changing conditions in medieval Europe including the organisation of city governments, the rise of lawyer and merchant classes, new national states, the new knowledge, the development of printing and the rise of Christian humanism made a break-up of the medieval world order inevitable. The complex series of economic, social and religious events known in shorthand as the Reformation brought to the fore the issue of freedom of religious worship and teaching. The right to freedom in religious belief which Luther claimed could not be denied to others, with the result that Protestantism, like a mirror smashing into a thousand pieces, witnessed massive and ongoing fragmentation which paradoxically contained the seeds both of its vitality and its destruction. It witnessed the rise of many competing denominations in the quest for religious purity, the elusive crock at the end of the Protestant rainbow. But with its increased emphasis on the individual believers' freedom of judgement and personal responsibility, not least in reading the Scripture for themselves, Protestantism brought also an impulse to mass education. Since Scripture, rather than the teaching of the Church, was held by Protestants to contain 'all things necessary to salvation', the Bible had to be made accessible to the people.

Protestantism was restrained in England by the muted appearance of the Reformation in the form of the Church of England, among reformed churches one of the closest to the contemporary Roman Catholic church. The abolition of the song, chantry and hospital schools left a large gap in elementary education. Christianity came to be identified with strict conformity to the principles of the established church and schools were expected to conform within this process. The Pandora's box of freedom to question had been opened, however, and short periods of savage persecution could not stifle alternative views. The serious attention to the discussion of religious matters, such as that evidenced in the UK in the seventeenth century, required a level of literacy sufficient to read the Bible and the vitriolic writings of the religious pamphleteers: Baptists, Fifth Monarchy Men, Muggletonians, Quakers etc. So having reduced the education provision in the UK by closing what was seen as under Roman control, Protestantism paradoxically increased the need for it. This was in contrast to some states, such as Calvin's Geneva, which had introduced free, universal, elementary education in the vernacular in the three Rs, along with religion (Christianity) and citizenship. The religious and spiritual aspects of education remained as obvious as they had done prior to the Reformation. It was assumed that there was a 'fourth R'. But the response to the growing educational need in the UK also reflected the parsimony which came to characterise UK education investment over centuries. The dame school, a local, usually rudimentary and cheap form of introduction to reading and writing, and the religious charity school, left to philanthropy on the part of organisations like the Society for the Propagation of Christian Knowledge (founded 1699), evidenced a reluctance by government to be involved in mass education. UK education was emerging with a strong tradition of voluntarism instead of state provision, and a set of largely unquestioned Protestant assumptions.

The eighteenth-century legacy in UK education

New types of intellectual enquiry and in particular the developments in science led to a progressive reduction in supernaturalism as a way of solving unanswered questions about the world or events within it. New philosophical, scientific and economic concerns began to overtake theology as the uppermost issues for intelligent debate. Rousseau's view that people were not obliged to submit to government against their wills and his championship of universal suffrage were not merely extensions of the Protestant principle and highly influential in the French Revolution; they stemmed from a view of personhood which was to have a continuing effect on education for centuries. Rousseau rejected the prevailing theories of middle- and upper-class education, which made children conform to adult norms, dress and behaviour patterns, on pain of harsh disciplinary enforcement procedures; he offered instead a view which accepted the autonomy of the child. Education should fit the child's growing capacities, should take place through the senses rather than the memory, should abandon the study of 'theological subtleties', should utilise the natural interests, curiosities and activities of children, should embrace conversation, drawing, music and play, be many-sided rather than monochrome, and should develop a reasoning individual, capable of directing their life. There were massive flaws in Rousseau's thesis and methodology: he used a fictitious case study; it was a single child and not a class of thirty; it was developed within a context of a repressive contemporary religious instructional model and was a reaction to that. But Rousseau opened up a different potential for the notion of spiritual development, not as hitherto the inculcation of spiritual truths as defined by creed, dogma or formula, but as something within the individual persona, psychology and nature of the child. It was at once a Romantic view combined with an increasingly secular development of the Protestant principle, to be taken further by Bonhoeffer in his view of humankind come of age.

All this was an eighteenth-century legacy, but it was not to be greatly in evidence in the UK until the twentieth century. Here it was manifest not only in 'child-centred' theories of education in the 1960s, which produced extreme 'free schools' like Dartington Hall and also affected mainstream classroom practice, but in the more mature version that emerged in the 1970s and afterwards of 'child-related' teaching and learning. Distorted in some presentations of spirituality, child-centredness was to present itself as a 'narcissistic flight from social engagement' (J. Elias, in Myers, 1997: 88), or as a naivety that sees humankind as better than they are, or as an absorption with the present. It is possible to interpret spiritual development post-1988 as one of the few surviving 'child-centred' activities within a centralised curriculum dominated by 'subjects' and 'facts' and testing.

The identification of Christianity as a 'religion'

Another of the developments that was to follow the French Revolution was the increasing perception that Christianity was a religion, albeit seen as the most advanced of its species and the formative force behind 'civilisation', i.e. European civilisation. It was no longer an assumed and all-embracing world-view. In time this was to lead to consideration of the evolution of religions (Troeltsch *et al.*) with the implicit assumption that higher forms of religion might be evolving, or that perhaps religion itself as a 'species' or type could decline and disappear. It also contained the questions that were to burst in later Victorian time and beyond: on what basis if any could one assert the superiority of one religion against another? How could one resolve conflicting truth claims? There was also a growing tendency to assume that all 'religions' could fit the same sort of framework and therefore be compared.

Some, such as Hinduism, were given a name and identity in this process, like labelling a newly discovered plant genus. This was a major shift from the often unconscious assumption which had been held well into the eighteenth century that Christianity was the truth about life, or that Hinduism was 'sanatan dharma'. Many people were unable to distinguish the frame of reference which religion was being presented in from the complex, changing and living traditions that were subsumed in this way.

Moreover it is possible that centuries of Christian quarrels about doctrine had helped to establish another assumption about Christianity: that its essence was belief rather than praxis. It was to lead to a twentieth-century European tendency to identify religions with belief systems to which one might choose to subscribe, or not. Thus, very significantly, religion began to be seen as an *option*, even a *pastime*, and religions began to be seen as *institutions* or even *clubs*, which individuals might or might not join. If one could join honestly, one might; if not, personal integrity was deemed to require an agnostic or an atheistic stance. In an age of uncertainties, religion was presented as something for the certain. Doubt was held to be its antithesis, a state of mind that required one to discard the pretence of religion. Thus by the late nineteenth century, individual conscience and integrity became higher authorities than religions or denominations or creeds. Religions ceased to be seen as world-views and in place arose a secular world-view, of which people were far less aware, within which religion was subsumed and domesticated as a minority option. It was a loss of credibility for religion, which was publicised from Bonhoeffer onwards. But theologians were torn as to whether to welcome this process with Bonhoeffer, van Buren and Cupitt, or whether to attempt to fight it. Even religious educators began to semi-apologise for the name 'religion' in their subject title; Acland, for example, wanted to call it 'Religion and Life'. But such titles accepted the severance of the two in the popular mind and implied that the task of the religious educator was somehow to demonstrate the relevance of religion to what was assumed to be the real, i.e. the religionless, world. One CSE examination course replaced RE in its title with 'The Art of Living', a galimatias of a phrase, no less free of semantic difficulty.

This reduction of religion along with a parallel tendency, the tendency to see religion as divisive in a society in which increasingly atheists, secular humanists, agnostics, and people of quite differing religious affiliations co-existed, meant that compulsory religious observance (such as that in school worship, in contrast to the rise of religious *education* in the classroom, which did not attempt to conscript belief) became increasingly problematic. It seemed that the majority, non-worshippers, were being compelled towards the practice of the minority and the minority were increasingly less willing to defend the morality of this situation. When the Evangelical Alliance recognised the great difficulties posed by compulsory school worship and, while not supporting total abolition, did not see school worship simply as an opportunity for missionary endeavour, it was a sign of the complexity that was acknowledged by all sides.

Meanwhile the inner uncertainties, residual superstitions, beliefs, aspirations, longings, and half-articulated convictions of the many were not being addressed in education. If many teachers were happy to discard compulsory religious worship and could tell stories of their unhappy encounters with religious institutions such as Sunday schools in their own childhood, they were prepared to acknowledge the less divisive term 'spiritual' as covering a part of the human condition that should be addressed. The scene was set for attention to be turned to exploring the 'spiritual' (or was it perhaps the authentically religious?) longing of humankind. But in espousing the notion of the spiritual, they were turning to a phrase which, like religion, carried its own history and conglomerate meanings. Some of these have been identified in the Introduction, but we now re-examine a number in more detail, in the context of their originating thinkers.

Spirituality as part of the human condition?
S.T. Coleridge (1772–1834)

Coleridge remains an enduring and seminal thinker, whose attitudes towards the Bible and spirituality were transposed into the education system through Thomas Arnold, who added his own distinctive interpretations to both (see pp. 29–32). The legacy of both men has formed a largely forgotten background to the development of attitudes towards the spiritual in UK schools. Both men were personally acquainted with Wordsworth and knew his work. As in the case of trying to recover the 'real' Arnold (p. 20f), but for different reasons, it is not an easy task to reconstruct the authentic Coleridge, partly because of 'a seemingly infinite elasticity of evidence' (Fruman, 1971: 3) about Coleridge, but more because of his incomplete and prolific writings which sometimes represent half-formed or changing points of view, often seminal and mercurial.

Coleridge held that the spiritual was an integral dimension of being human: 'If there be aught *Spiritual* in Man, the Will must be such. *If* there be a Will, there must be a Spirituality in Man' (*Aids to Reflection*, 1825, 1993 edition: 135, emphases his and in following quotations). Coleridge was influenced by Boehme, Spinoza and Goethe (the latter also much influenced Matthew Arnold). It was hardly surprising that he was to find awareness of mystery another important attribute for humankind. He quoted an anonymous Schoolman with approval: 'Omnia exeunt in mysterium' (ibid.: 139). Coleridge shunned metaphysical 'proofs' of religious truth in favour of pragmatic and empirically derived experience: 'For all knowledge being derived from the Senses, the closer men are kept to the fountain head, the *knowinger* [*sic*] they must become' (*On the Constitution of Church and State*, 1830, 1976 edition: 62); 'Knowledge of spiritual Truth is of necessity immediate and intuitive' (*Aids to Reflection*, 1825, 1993 edition: 158). As early as 1816 he had distinguished three kinds of religion: religion 'comprehended in intellectuality [*sic*]', which was 'Philosophy for the few'; religion 'actualised in the feelings, but not comprehended in intellectuality', which was 'religion for the many'; finally 'the Symbolical forms by which Philosophy becomes Religion when instead of being actualised they are realised (into real Beings or forms having an essence or essential virtue of themselves)', which constitute superstition—a disease, according to Coleridge (*Shorter Works*, 1995 edition: I, 776). As in so many other ways, Coleridge was incisive in identifying that not all religion was good; that mass religion, which the late twentieth century sometimes preferred to call spirituality, was felt intuitively rather than believed in doctrine and formulae; and that 'intellectuality' had a bearing on religious conception.

This in his view had implications for curriculum. Coleridge proposed reading, writing, arithmetic, 'the mechanic arts', and a study of 'the elements and results of physical science'. He crossed out from an earlier draft 'experimental philosophy' as an added subject. Coleridge was not alone. William Blake (1757–1827) argued that the Bible would be found more entertaining and instructive when it was realised that it was addressed to the imagination, not to reason or understanding. The child is the measure of all good and the intrinsic qualities of childhood reveal how far humankind has moved from eternal values. Dogma and institutional religion can victimise children. Blake replaced Rousseau's primitive nobility of childhood with an angelic simplicity. For Blake the world of imagination was the world of eternity. The poet's task was a religious one, to mediate divine revelations to humankind. Children could glimpse it. The tasks of the poet and the theologian are inseparable. However, Blake was to have less influence on education than Coleridge, because Coleridge was hailed posthumously as the father of the broad church mood in the Church of England, an approach to the Bible and theology which was to become dominant by the end of the nineteenth century. Unlike Blake, Coleridge was translated and adapted by Arnold into the education system, and through Arnold and the Arnold cult on to new generations of headteachers, cascading from public schools to grammar schools and on to aspiring elementary and later secondary modern schools. Blake in contrast scarcely survived, in educational terms, except as the author of the poems 'The Tyger' and 'Jerusalem'. The latter was sung as a hymn in school worship by generations of children who were rarely if at all inducted into its meaning. It may be noted *en passant* with Blake, however, that the tendency among commentators has been to ignore the contributions that poets might have made to spiritual development and focus instead on philosophers. Some poets, e.g. Brooke, could be said to have been abused to fit state-sponsored spiritualities, such as the glorification of war and the idea of the 'glorious dead' (see pp. 48ff).

Spirit as a potential in human existence:
Søren Kierkegaard (1813–55)

Kierkegaard's writings became influential in England only in the twentieth century, as a result of their late translation from the original Danish and when, against his own wishes, he began to be seen as the father of a new school or mood of thought, existentialism. Given his implacable opposition to Bishop Mynster and the Danish established church, and his notion of the injurious concept of Christendom, resulting in the churches' reduction of Christianity to a mass hobby, it is hard to imagine that Kierkegaard would ever have sanctioned the state propagation of spirituality through the curriculum. It would have seemed to him anathema. Through his writings and particularly the journals, his view of the spiritual can be constructed. The starting point is a survival of the Hegelianism he rejected in so many other ways:

> Man is a synthesis. He is both an animal creation and the possibility of spirit. But the animal needs no higher certainty than numbers. To feel the impulse to another kind of certainty than that of numbers introduces spirit. (*Journal: The Last Years*, 1854, 1965 translation: 163).

This dualism continues in Kierkegaard's assertion that the life of the senses and the life of the spirit are opposites and that spirit is 'the will to die, the will to die to the world' (ibid.: 178). The bitter conflict between the natural person and the spirit is more a feature of his later writings, when much bitter conflict had been part of his life. For Kierkegaard, the lack of spirit is the way to make life easy and the material person understands this well. In contrast is his celebrated view of the *engelte*, variously translated as 'single person' or 'solitary individual', the only authentic existence open to a person. But Protestant Christianity has so abandoned this path that it has progressed backwards, under the same sort of self-treatment that in a contemporary Danish comedy led the doctor to pronounce 'the patient is dead, but the fever has entirely vanished' (ibid.: 196).

Number is part of Kierkegaard's understanding of spirit:

> One hundred thousand million men, of which each is like the rest = one. Only when one turns up who is different from these millions or this one, do we have two. In the world of numbers it is unity which counts; in the world of the spirit unity does not count, because difference counts, which means that there is no counting ... For 'spirit' everything is reversed. In the world of sense one adds up, and it becomes a large number, in the world of spirit one adds up and the large number vanishes as in a conjuring trick ... (ibid.: 230f.)

Spirit is thus a form of self-differentiation (ibid.: 245) in contrast to the factory-made conformity of state Christianity. But for Kierkegaard the spirit is also fire; Christianity is 'incendiarism'. It is a fire of purification which is internal. By a 'diabolical ingenuity' the burning of early Christians reflected this externally, bringing to mind the words of Jesus: 'I came to cast fire upon the earth' (ibid.: 205f.). In contrast to this requirement for lonely suffering, most of humankind are happy to live in a herd, in which a person is a social animal whose only distinguishing characteristic from non-human animals is the possession of envy.

The spirit is also unrest. It has been tamed, however. The difficulty people have with the New Testament teaching about dying to the world as part of life in the spirit is 'resolved' by using biblical commentaries that explain it away, to soften the blow. Christians, he notes, have a historic tendency to make difficult biblical texts easy, so as to avoid their import. Kierkegaard states that if the New Testament taught that every person should have $100,000, we would quickly throw away our commentaries, in case they cast doubt on the text (ibid.: 334f.). In his last journal entry (24 September 1855), Kierkegaard writes of the examination of life, in which those without spirit merely cling to life and those with it reach a point of disgust with life. God favours the latter, because they do not in the end believe in themselves, but in God.

Commenting, Arbaugh and Arbaugh (1968: 300ff.) argue that for Kierkegaard, the self is spirit, that which freely, responsibly and inwardly selects values and sets the course of life. A self is not a static being but an active becoming, in which the relation between finitude and infinitude perpetuates itself. Spirit comes into being in the act whereby humankind relates itself to God, and this encounter generates personal values. There is a common spiritual sickness, in which a self may lose itself, or fail to possess itself, or despair of self. The most common form of worldliness is despair, to be unconscious of oneself as spirit. This can even arise when a person seeks to be too spiritual and dreams too much, with no concrete actuality, volatising the self in possibility, not the now. Without God, humankind has no enduring self and lacks the possibility of spirit. But it is a mistake to develop a theological system of apologetics: one cannot make rationally acceptable that which lies beyond rationality. It is prayer that establishes humankind's existence as spirit, enabling a person to cope with the tension between finite and infinite.

Clearly Kierkegaard does not impinge on views of spiritual development current in UK education. If anything he savages them by implication as pleasant self-explorations or vacuous dreaming. He has not shaped the way in which the educational debate in this field has been conducted, but that might be to its detriment.

Kierkegaard appears, as so often he must have done in life, as the unwelcome guest at the banquet. Yet the non-addressing of the issues he wishes to force people to face has enabled a comfortable, reassuring, therapeutic view of spiritual development to dominate the field. If his own view can be said to be morbid and extreme, the alternative in education might be said to be so tame and pain free that it may not provide help in time of trouble. Yet if we are to attempt taxonomies of spirituality, the classic spiritualities have provided this sort of help.

The numinous as a religious and spiritual experience: Rudolf Otto (1869–1937)

Otto was to exercise a formative but posthumous influence on the development of what became known in UK RE as experiential learning, for example on the team-produced book, *New Methods in RE Teaching* (Hammond *et al.*, 1990) (see p. 98f). But the influence of his thought in the evolving concepts of the spiritual in the curriculum can also be seen, in particular the notions of awe and wonder and his concept of the numinous. This was a remarkable legacy for a German Lutheran pastor and Professor of Theology whose own main work, *Das Heilige*, had been written in 1917, translated into English in 1923 as *The Idea of the Holy*, and who had no particular interest in school education or curriculum. Otto was, by the standards of his time or any since, enormously widely travelled. His visits included Alexandria, Burma, Cairo, Ceylon, China, Corfu, Finland, France, the Greek mainland, India, Italy, North Africa, Japan, Palestine, Russia, Sweden, Trieste, the USA, the UK and Venice. He observed at first hand and read widely about Buddhism including Japanese Zen, Coptic Christians, Dervishes, Greek Orthodox monastic life, various aspects of Hinduism, Islam, Italian Roman Catholicism, Jainism, Moroccan Judaism, Parseeism, Russian Orthodoxy, Taoism and Theosophy. He attended the second World Missionary Conference in Jerusalem in 1928 along with William Temple. An austere and rather unapproachable man as seen by his students at Marburg, with a tendency to depression, Otto's formal and rather military bearing presented an impression, wrongly, of coldness. His tragic death following a fall from a tower was wrapped in the same awesome mystery that was part of his persona and interpretation of religion.

Otto's work was out of fashion theologically in the Barthian climate of his time, but it was to prove as endurable as Barthianism and to have more implications for religious education and spiritual development. His travels not only reflected a deep interest in the religious experience of humankind but also confronted him with questions that many scholars did not face until the rise of multi-religious populations after the Second World War. Was one of these religions superior to others? If so, by what criteria could such a religion be identified? Was there some sort of religious 'essence' that underlay them all? How could one schematise the massively diverse expressions of religious emotion and experience, if at all? Moreover there was the issue in all religions of the balance between the rational—expressed in creeds, dogma, theologies—and the non-rational. There was also the danger of the irrational, in fundamentalism and fanaticism. Did religions provide a balance between their rational elements and their non-rational elements? Raphael has noted that Otto's style was more evocative than analytic and that as a Lutheran he assumed religion to be primarily an inner experience; for him religious impulses had affinities with moral and emotional impulses (Raphael, 1997: 19, 24).

The tendency in theology and comparative religion studies, Otto argued, was to show bias towards the rational and to ignore the non-rational. His self-appointed task was to explore the non-rational aspect of religion, although methodologically he recognised that this had to be carried through largely by means of rational discourse. Otto was forced to invent or alter language, or to leave language untranslated in order to express nuances and meanings that could not be supplied in standard terminology. His writing is littered with untranslated Aramaic, Greek, Hebrew, Latin, Sanskrit and (in the English version) German phrases that cannot be rendered into suitable English. One of his favourite biblical passages was, significantly, Isaiah Chapter 6.

By analogy with omen and ominous, Otto coined the word numinous from the Latin numen. The numinous was a mental state, *sui generis* and irreducible to any other. It had distinguishable elements: creature-feeling; *mysterium tremendum* including elements of awefulness, overpoweringness, energy ('wrath'), wholly-otherness and fascination. The numinous feeling is evoked by various means: the primitive, even loathsome aspect; terror and dread; grandeur and sublimity. These can be expressed in art or sculpture, by a building or place, by music, sound (like the Hindu Om), by silence and darkness. The holy for Otto has been overlaid with later ideas of morality and goodness. It is in itself the basis of all religion. In a letter from Mogador in 1911 he wrote:

> It is Sabbath, and already in the dark and inconceivably grimy passage of the house we hear that sing-song of prayers and reading of scripture, that nasal half-singing half-speaking which Church and Mosque have taken over from the Synagogue ... One can soon distinguish certain modulations and cadences that follow one another ... like *leitmotive*. The ear tries to grasp individual words, but it is scarcely possible and one has almost given up the attempt when suddenly out of the babel of voices, causing *a thrill of fear* [my italics], there it begins, unified, clear and unmistakable: Kadosh, Kadosh, Kadosh, Elohim, Adonai Zebaoth Male'u hashamayim wahaarets kebodo! (Holy, holy, holy, Lord God of Hosts, the heavens and the earth are full of your glory) ... In whatever language they resound, these most exalted words ... always grip one in the depths of the soul, with a mighty shudder exciting and calling into play the mystery of the other world latent therein. (in Turner, 1974: 4)

Otto charts the holy in Old and New Testaments, in Luther, in Indian religions, in cruder and more refined phases. Significantly in an editorial appendix on the numinous in English, John Harvey finds echoes of the demonic in Coleridge's 'Kubla Khan' (Otto, 1958 edition: 216), Blake's 'Tyger', Wordsworth's *Prelude*, F.W. Robertson and Isaac Watts.

In identifying an area or dimension of experience which purported to be acultural and to transcend particular religions, Otto himself was in no personal doubt about the superiority of Christianity. But he unwittingly created a base for later religious educators to use as a means to relate some of the inner feelings and experiences of their pupils to some of what Smart was to call the religious experience of humankind. As Otto explored the non-rational in religions, he opened the way for teachers to help children to explore their own non-rational experiences and aspirations and to relate these to the experiences of world religions. Otto thus became an inspiration for RE in the 1970s and 1980s. In the sense that the child's self was invited to engage in the process, which was not merely the rational learning about creeds or acquiring religious vocabulary or describing the outward actions of believers, it offered the potential for personal development. One can be less sure that Otto would have accepted that such an engagement by children would *de facto* create or enable spiritual development. For him we might develop spiritually as we become aware of or respond to the numen. But he took the view that numinous experience could be disturbing, even terrifying. What was planned for classrooms was necessarily more sanitised and teacher-controlled. For Otto in the end, the numen can never be controlled. It is *sui generis*. In this sense his influence on education was based on a careful filtering of what he had written. Unexpurgated, Otto would have produced a more vibrant and—from the point of view of the political establishment in education—dangerous type of spiritual development.

C.S. Lewis (1898–1963)

The spirituality of the Lewis circle: Anglican influence beyond the Anglican church

Although a Professor of Medieval and Renaissance English, 'Jack' Lewis is popularly remembered for his books for children and his Christian apologetics couched in easily understood language. Lewis, along with Charles Williams (1886–1945) and J.R.R. Tolkien (1892–1973), was part of a group of writers whose concern was with Christian transcendentalism in poetry and the language of symbol. Williams was a High Anglican as well as a member of a mystical semi-occult group. It is important to note that among their contemporaries were William Temple, Dorothy Sayers (whose influence as a leading Anglican lay person has been largely forgotten), T.S. Eliot and Richard Acland. Acland's Common Wealth Party, although eclipsed in the 1945 general election, held for many the hope of a democratic, Christian socialist alternative to Labour. Acland himself had a passionate commitment to education and had spoken in the 1943 Commons debate on the education bill, the only major piece of domestic legislation introduced by the government during the war (see pp. 66ff and Copley, 1997: 71–5). Christianity, and especially Anglican Christianity, was a high-profile concern in the 1940s, with both intellectual and popular standing, even if churchgoing remained a minority activity and the intellectual base was under attack from more recent schools of philosophy. Sayers provoked a storm with *The Man Born To Be King*, a series of radio plays originally broadcast live, which were an attempt to bring dramatic realism to the gospel and dispel the odour of piety that had surrounded it in previous productions. Her use of an actor to play the part of Christ caused controversy. But she was also prepared to satirise the church from the inside:

> Q: What does the Church call Sin?
> A: Sex ...; getting drunk; saying 'damn'; murder and cruelty to dumb animals; not going to church; most kinds of amusement. 'Original sin' means that anything that we enjoy doing is wrong. (in Coomes, 1992: 132)

Writing in wartime, she was anxious 'to remind people of the spiritual aims for which it [the war] is waged' and to 'stimulate enjoyment in spiritual and mental exercise' (ibid.: 157). From 1943 she studied the spirituality of Dante. Sayers was sufficiently acceptable to the Anglican hierarchy to be offered a Lambeth DD which she declined, perhaps because of fear that the consequent inevitable media interest might discover her illegitimate son.

It was in this context of creative Christian concern and growing ecumenism that the 1944 educational settlement evolved and out of which the post-war tradition of spiritual development also evolved. But by virtue of his popular writing for children, Lewis was to prove the most enduring of this Christian group. Sayers lived on as a detective writer, but not as a Christian apologist, despite *The Mind of The Maker*. Williams and Temple disappeared from public view. Acland remained a lone idealist, resigning even from Labour when the party accepted the H bomb, but making a brief impact on RE in the 1960s. Lewis lived on in children's fiction for generations, his works transposing into television in the process. Among those on whom he exercised a deep influence, 'the most impact on my intellectual religious formulation', was the undergraduate Margaret Thatcher, who ascribed his influence in part to his accessibility of language and his wittiness in writing (Thatcher, 1995: 40f.).

Lewis's Christianity
Lewis traced his own spiritual progress from 'popular realism' via philosophical Idealism then pantheism on to theism and finally Christianity. He described it as a natural but rarely trodden path

(1933: 5). While distinguishing seven confusing meanings of the word romantic, he described himself as a romantic in the sense of one involved on a quest that embraces intense longing, a mysterious and unattainable object of desire which leads to journeying and yet for which to desire is in some sense to have (ibid.: 8ff.). He had experienced two 'conversions' which were public knowledge, one to theism in 1929, which occurred on a bus in Oxford, and a later one to Christianity in 1931, on a journey to Whipsnade Zoo. Both events had complex antecedents which Lewis could identify. The conversions were conscious recognitions of what had occurred. He came to Christianity by a Neo-Platonic assumption of the sense of another world, of heaven being penetrable by dreams, the subconscious and the imagination (Wilson, 1990: 137). He was influenced by Inge. Tolkien, Lewis's influential friend at the time of his conversion to Christianity and himself a Roman Catholic, believed that truth was best discerned through myth.

Lewis had read almost no biblical scholarship, nor was he familiar with the latest philosophy of his professorial contemporary at Cambridge, Wittgenstein. He could see by 1943 that philosophy inhabited another world from the Idealism in which he had been reared. As a Christian apologist, Lewis's work stems really from the 1930s and 1940s and tends towards dualism, as in *Screwtape*, which presupposes a Devil. His real contribution to Christian apologetic was to come through his imaginative writing, not his intellectual discourse. In his fiction, Lewis's central characters develop a new spiritual awareness of the universe by a process of personal experience, moving from ignorant agnosticism to wonder and belief. The universe for him is one of extraordinary complexity and richness, yet also luminous clarity, with subtleties of artistic design and effect (Manlove, 1987: 6). It contains a strange current of joy, *Sehnsucht*, which has no identifiable object except heaven. For Lewis, literary richness reflected the expression of a corresponding spiritual richness; in this he had common ground with Matthew Arnold. Story is not merely a vehicle for truth; it can *be* truth.

Lewis's fiction created other worlds as a sort of imaginative enrichment of creation. He had a sense of the numinous. His seven Narnia books, which were to prove so popular among post-war children and later generations, and were serialised on television in the 1980s and 1990s, were all written between 1950 and 1956:

The Lion, the Witch and the Wardrobe (1950), *Prince Caspian* (1951), *The Voyage of the 'Dawn Treader'* (1952), *The Silver Chair* (1953), *The Horse and His Boy* (1954), *The Magician's Nephew* (1955) and *The Last Battle* (1956). They are reflections of Christian values and parabolic or allegorical teaching in Britain at the time. But they were written against a human backcloth of the decline and death of Lewis's long-time friend 'Minto' Moore, the alcoholism of his brother Warnie and the cooling of long-established friendships at Oxford. Perhaps this is why he was a person with no time for small talk, nor did he discuss personal matters in conversation. The Narnia books deal with the interpenetration of worlds and 'the England within England', a world where 'no good thing is destroyed'.

Lewis believed that there was a spirituality or a spiritual receptor in humankind:

> Human life has always been lived on the edge of a precipice ... [People] ... propound mathematical theorems in beleaguered cities, conduct metaphysical arguments in condemned cells, make jokes on scaffolds, discuss the last new poem while advancing to the walls of Quebec, and comb their hair at Thermopylae. This is not *panache*: it is our nature. (in Berger, 1970: 77)

In a sermon he stated that 'almost our whole education has been directed to silencing this shy, persistent, inner voice [that points beyond a this-worldly view]', which he calls a 'longing for the transtemporal' (Lewis, 1962: 201). Nor is it mere aestheticism. 'We do not merely want to *see* beauty [his italics] ... We want something else which can hardly be put into words—to be united with the beauty we see, to pass into it, to receive it into ourselves, to bathe in it, to become part of it' (ibid.: 208). It is a mystic communion. But 'a man whose mind was formed in a period of cynicism and disillusion, cannot teach hope or fortitude ... As the teachers are, so they will teach' (in Sandhurst, 1948: 9ff.).

At the same time, he was willing to focus on the development of the individual, something which was to make him relevant in the world of the 1960s and beyond:

> Every time you make a choice you are turning the central part
> of you, the part of you that chooses, into something a little

different from what it was before. And taking your life as a whole, with all your innumerable choices, all your life you are slowly turning this central thing into either a heavenly creature or a hellish creature. (Lewis, *Mere Christianity*: 83)

There has been a system of values, from earliest literature to the present day, outside individual feelings and the utilitarian requirements of society, a generally accepted standard of right and wrong, that cuts across religions. Lewis called it the Tao. The Tao accepts that humankind is moral and spiritual. But recent invention of value systems in Nazi Germany and Russia are dangerous attempts to manipulate or extinguish the Tao. Although Lewis's defence of Christianity and Christian values was not intellectually influential in the world of the university, it carried popular appeal through his writing.

Lewis made no attempt systematically to apply his ideas to education. But he offered not so much a spirituality without pain (Kierkegaard's was too frightening) or one without dread (Otto's could be unpleasant, even gruesome; he coined the term grue) but one which was in the end good. Mr Beaver described Aslan as not safe, but good. The English were susceptible to the appeal of goodness, especially when recently engaged in a war which some couched in apocalyptic terms as the struggle for human survival against totalitarian alternatives. It provided the happy ending that people desired: good triumphed, not without pain, but its final triumph was absolute. This could easily subvert into a popular universalism: it need not matter what you believed, or even did, as all things would turn out all right in the end. For many, good mattered more than God. They did not see them as indissolubly linked, as in Platonism. This adaptation, or perhaps distortion, of Lewis could marry an optimistic view of human development to produce a view of spiritual development which was optimistic, benign and sufficiently vague to be applied to education without too much controversy.

Ludwig Wittgenstein (1889–1951)

Wittgenstein's life experiences in Austria, in studying mechanical engineering in Berlin and Manchester, in work on reaction jet propellers in aeronautics, in service in the artillery, including the trenches in the First World War, as a prisoner of war in Italy (completing the only work of his to be published in his life-time), in the study of mathematical logic, as a Cambridge academic, as a hospital porter in the Second World War, and as a recluse, have in common with Coleridge and Kierkegaard a strong atypicality. They reveal an academic incompleteness and at times disregard, even disdain, for the written record. Like Coleridge and Kierkegaard, Wittgenstein has also been used by others to justify their positions, not always appropriately. Extreme caution is needed in attempting to avoid similar misuse in this context. Wittgenstein does not so much address the spiritual in detail as make a number of remarks in other contexts which have implications for an understanding of the spiritual in education. The first is a reverential approach: 'It is not *how* things are in the world that is mystical, but *that* it exists' (*Tractatus*, 6.44); 'There are indeed, things that cannot be put into words. They make themselves manifest. They are what is mystical' (ibid.: 6.522). The last sentence of the *Tractatus* is also deeply reverential: 'of what one cannot speak, thereof one must be silent'. Reverence, however, is coupled with openness: 'In every serious philosophical question, uncertainty extends to the very roots of the problem. We must always be prepared to learn something totally new' (*Remarks on Colour*: Section 15). Talk of the spiritual is not entirely ruled out: 'Where our language suggests a body and there is none: there, we should like to say, is a spirit' (*Philosophical Investigations*: Section 36). In aesthetics, appreciation is not a mere response; it relates to patterns, 'rules', traditions of composition and comment, the degree of imitativeness in the object. But it is impossible to describe what appreciation consists of. What belongs to a language game is a whole culture. What we now call a cultured taste probably did not exist in the Middle Ages. To describe what is meant by a cultured taste, one has to describe a culture. To become clear about aesthetic words it is necessary to describe ways of living. Aesthetic questions are difficult because they are not susceptible to empirical answers (Wittgenstein, 1966: 6–11, 17f.). By implication, to talk of the spiritual and of spiritual development one has to describe a culture setting and be clear about the language game being used. Such clarity has not yet been found. Wittgenstein is providing a reminder of what the development of 'spiritual development' ignored: that it takes place within a culture context which needs to be thoroughly understood.

Some implications for education

Myers (1997: 101f.) argues that spirit is a biological condition of being human. But 'at this point in our understanding of human development, that which ignites spirit remains a mystery'. All human beings in every culture, she argues, have spirit as a life-giving force. Spirit fuels transcendence, hope and the ability to learn, but it does not do these automatically. She writes as two boys aged ten and eleven are being sentenced for dropping a five-year-old out of a fourteenth-floor window because he refused to steal candy for them. It was a US equivalent to the James Bulger killing in the UK (1993). For Myers it is an issue that leads to the heart of spirituality and how a society acknowledges and encourages it: 'When our children become our enemies, where is hope?' She cites Fowler's view that faith can be a relational dynamic in which people may claim a centre, or centres, of value and power in their lives. She argues that this can be achieved within the education process. But can it? Is the secular education process salvific?

In the final chapter we have to try to make sense of the disparate and incomplete traditions of spiritual development that have been transposed into the education system in the UK. What has been demonstrated in this chapter is that compared with the writings of some philosophers, the tendency to sanitise and secularise spiritual development within the UK education system, to render it a benign, consensus-driven, self-exploratory process, at pains to offend no one, is based on a philosophical platform (and borrowing from popular culture, e.g. Lewis) which has been both selective and weak. It has edited out first the Christian, then the 'broadly Christian' influences of some of the thinkers above and also those who appeared in earlier chapters. It has tamed tigers. But in the end it will be found to satisfy neither the perceptions and experiences of different world religions nor the more radical view of the secularist, who could quite easily continue the present reduction process by moving beyond the current broadly spiritual path and into either moral development or citizenship, neither of which requires transcendence or mystery. School worship has all but been abandoned as a defensible compulsory activity for the county, i.e. non-church, school. The current view of spiritual development could follow. Worship has to be religious to be credible as worship, but in society in which compulsory religion is unacceptable, the future of compulsory school worship may be bleak. Spiritual development has dispensed with its religious, i.e. originally Christian, base in order to become acceptable among the communities of education. But in so doing it may have ceased to be spiritual in any sense which has continuity with UK or world religions traditions of understanding spiritual. It may have survived by ceasing to be—a strange sort of survival.

Conclusion

The Place of the Spiritual in
UK Education in a New Millennium

The hijack of 'spiritual development' by a secular humanist rationale?

The place of the spiritual in UK education has roots that go back at least to pre-Reformation times (p. 110f). As the churches could no longer afford to be the sole providers of schools and the population exploded, non-religiously financed schools spread rapidly. They still retained, largely by popular consent if not positive desire, provision for the spiritual within the curriculum and as a ritual or token recognition of widely (but never universally) accepted values in the form of a daily act of worship. One conclusion of this enquiry is that a consistent line of development of the tradition of the spiritual can be traced in English and Welsh education up to the 1960s and early 1970s, but that discontinuity occurs then as a result of the collapse of a consensus on Christian values for education. This collapse was brought about by a complex of factors including individualism; a consumer-oriented culture; secularisation; mass awareness of the pluralism of religions; the acceptability and sometimes apparent fashion of atheistic life-stances; widespread relativism culminating in a pervasive assumption that the truth is whatever one chooses it be; the growing power of the media and of the alternative cultures of fashion and pop music; and major changes in family life and values. In the light of this complexity of powerful factors at work, the collapse of a commonly accepted Christian values-base would not easily be reversible, if at all, even if this were deemed desirable. The only possibility, sociologically, is that as in any religion, a new prophet may arise and an unforeseen revival may occur. With television, the Web and Information and Communicative Technology (ICT), the influence and following of such a person could spread with amazing rapidity. In trying to assess the near future we have to limit comment to what seems reasonably predictable, the probable, while not ruling out the possible. We have therefore to discard religious revival as a likely event, always with the proviso that one cannot be sure.

The political debate in the various legal settlements from 1870 is important for two key reasons. First, it reflects the voice and thinking of those with power, the legislators. In the UK, education legislation in this century may have been produced after consultation with education professionals and occasionally taking their views into account, but it has never been driven by professionals. An acute example of this is the position of worship in DfE Circular 1/94, which received immediate and widespread condemnation among the teaching profession. After the introduction of the National Curriculum (1988) politicians, led by secretaries of state for education, and associated curriculum quangos have even more power to inflict their or their political party's presuppositions about education upon the system. The arrival of the Teacher Training Agency with its power to de-license providers of initial teacher training, which gives it a hold over the universities it licenses, and the power given to Ofsted in applying the criteria for the inspection of teacher training courses meant that politicians and quango heads could take hold of the training process itself. First the curriculum, then the training of those who were to implement it, were taken under political control. The language of official documentation made clear the status of their subjects: 'trainers' and 'trainees' rather than teacher educators and intern teachers, for instance. 'Trainer' also implied the language of manuals and instruction, with the implication that the manual matters more, the trainer merely implements it. Significantly, a series of prescriptions began to emerge about the content of the training process beginning with core subjects, English, Mathematics and Science. This legislation had been originally enacted by a Conservative government in the name of wiping out left-wing dogmatism in curriculum and training courses, but the New Labour government of 1997 showed no sign that it was going to relax this hold. Spiritual development, as part of the curriculum, was thus placed into the hands of politicians. Yet nations do not naturally look to politicians for spiritual wisdom.

Seeing into the minds of the legislators is therefore an important part of understanding how spiritual development came to be where it is. The other reason why the legislation matters is that the politicians reflect lay views on the matter. Theirs may be unusually articulate and not always representative forms of lay views, but they are lay views nonetheless. In this field to restrict study to professional output and philosophical consideration would be to miss vital culture context clues provided by political debate and the subsequent legal provision. The nineteenth-century adage that 'we must educate our masters', i.e. the newly enfranchised masses, might now be reversed. Those concerned with RE and spiritual development have the uphill task of educating their 'masters', i.e. the politicians.

It has also been argued that although the philosophical bases for the nature of spirituality remain diffuse and do not lend themselves to exhaustive survey, particular people have made clearly identifiable contributions. Thus Thomas Arnold, who was not unique as an education manager in his headship role, was unusual in being able to test his philosophy of education in practice in a situation he could to a large extent control, Rugby School. He was unique in the influence he attained through his former pupils, his biographers, his imitators as heads, and the wide and often unnoticed influence of the Arnold dynasty, especially Jane via Forster, and Matthew. They did not merely copy his views, but adapted and developed them against the backcloth of a very changed late Victorian society.

Thomas Arnold's views on sin were part of a robust view of spiritual development which was strong enough to survive the Great War. But by then it was already a minority view, even within Christianity. The more fashionable liberal view of 'development' was ill-fitted to survive into the changed national psyche after the war. Yet amazingly it did survive two world wars and the Holocaust as far as education was concerned. One may wonder why. Perhaps it is the Micawber element in the human psyche that, despite all appearances, hopes that things will get better. For many, education was seen as an improving opportunity, a chance to 'get on', which promoted a liberal view of humankind. Or perhaps education had become too divorced from 'life' for the mismatch in views of a liberal humanistic view of progress and development to show up. Perhaps we do not learn from history. Perhaps liberal views of development were less dented by a succession of wars in which the English, despite every bungle and blunder from the Crimea onwards, always seemed to end up on the winning side; war memorials are mute reminders, which can easily be ignored, of the human price even of victory. Perhaps feelings of national grief were subsumed into festivals of remembrance. More likely is that a consumerist and individualistic society was happy to bury the unwelcome images of suffering, untimely death and war and the questions of meaning these raised, especially after fifty years of peace and relative prosperity on the UK mainland.

The picture for 'spiritual development' is more complex than one of residual institutional Christianity and a secular humanist alternative competing for domination in the education system. As Christianity became more internally plural in late Victorian times, it was possible for less credal, only broadly or vaguely Christian spiritualities based on Deism or reverence for life to assume more prominence. This had been the case in the eighteenth century until the Methodist revival. Unitarianism and the Labour churches were institutional examples of this tendency in Victorian England but there was a wider, diffusive Christianity, among many non-churchgoers. Robert Elsmere and Mark Rutherford were fictitious characters, so real to life as to be credible to many readers who knew their dilemmas and perhaps had sympathy with their outcomes. Both achieved peace not without pain but without, or even despite, orthodox Christianity. For some, the attachment to a 'broader' Christianity included church attendance at Christmas and harvest, but for others not at all, except perhaps for funerals. For others it was a Christianity of the sort C.S. Lewis inspired, a Christian sentiment or sympathy without any Christian institutional connection. These views ran alongside more traditional Christian views held by a minority and sowed some of the seeds of the present confused position in spiritual development in state schools. How far children after 1945 were influenced or affected by school worship and the presence of the spiritual within the state school system is an under-researched area and the answers must at present be largely conjectural.

After the Second World War, secularisation advanced in UK society very rapidly. The decline of churches, especially the Free Churches, continued, with ample architectural evidence in the form of chapel buildings converted to Sikh temples, carpet warehouses, desirable country residences etc. The Free Church practice of recording formal membership also demonstrates this steep decline. The Sunday school population among all churches collapsed. A generation of children who had been sent (rather than taken) to Sunday school by their parents did not bother to send their own children. Churches became more dynastic and inward-looking, preoccupied with the mending of denominational divisions. Sabbatarian legislation was gradually relaxed and then abandoned altogether to allow first widespread sport and entertainment and, later, unrestricted shopping. The out-of-town shopping complexes of the 1980s and 1990s took on the appearance of cathedrals of their age, symbolic palaces in a consumer-driven culture, providing food, fashion, furniture, finance, pharmaceuticals and even funerals. The car and the television changed the patterns of family behaviour and churchgoing. The National Lottery, despite use of the divine finger on early television advertisements and the banal prayer 'although I'm a sinner, make me a winner', was a symbol of the desire not for God but for material prosperity. It represented the mysterious power of money to change human destiny. Those using the Church of England for weddings, baptisms and funerals declined as a percentage of population. The 1994 Marriage Act allowed secular sites such as hotels, historic castles and football clubs to be licensed to conduct civil marriages. By May 1998 2,000 such sites had been licensed, including London Zoo. Some could rival the photogenic settings of churchyards. The provision has yet to be extended to funerals. In 1998 New Labour discussed the provision of secular pastoral counsellors, to fill a role which in another age had been provided by the clergy. The multi-ethnic urban populations were visible reminders that different cultures and religions were present, not simply in the world, but in the UK. Institutional Christianity began to be regarded as a minority preoccupation alongside other minorities. In schools the question arose whether there could be a unifying school culture or whether there could only be co-existing or, worse, competing cultures. Teachers on the whole wanted schools to be integrative communities that respected and affirmed diversity. Not all parents and politicians agreed. Some preferred separation. In this changed situation, it is easy to see why an essentially secular and different understanding of spirituality began to dominate, but its roots too were at least Victorian. It was not new.

Such shifts were made more easy by the changing use of

language already noted (pp. 1–6 and 15). It was something of an uncritical conglomerate on spirituality that emerged, but it was perhaps inevitable in so complex a society that spirituality should take on a complex of meanings. One of the most vigorous attacks on recent trends in spiritual development came from Adrian Thatcher. As Professor of Applied Theology at a Church of England College, he provided an unreservedly Christian commentary on the recent developments. To Thatcher, the growth in RE and spiritual development of the notion of the private self, the inner me, is deeply flawed. It has been discredited in philosophy by Ryle, Wittgenstein, Heidegger, Rorty, Foucault and others. Thatcher characterises recent western philosophy as the story of the rise and fall of the Self. But in recent RE, personal and social education and spiritual development, 'the self continues to rise' (Thatcher, 1991: 22). It is the culmination of a long process of the marginalisation of God and the outcome of a privatised religion in which each of us can decide what is real and everyone's experience has its own validity. Thatcher's concerns about the direction of spiritual development need not be interpreted as specifically Christian. A Muslim critique could be based on very similar lines, that 'spiritual development' is a liberal western construct, locked into a secular base of a multi-cultural society in which truth questions are avoided at all costs and the truth is merely what 'I' conceive it to be. Hay and Hammond defended their own work from attack by Thatcher (1992) by asserting that for them 'inner' is about depth as opposed to surface knowledge, that it is a metaphor for attentiveness, mindfulness, and that it does not depend on a dualistic view of humankind. Mott-Thornton (1996) also criticised Thatcher's interpretation of Wittgenstein. But these defences are not entirely convincing: a spirituality tailored to the supreme 'I' seems to be dominant within the processes of education.

The ineradicable problem of meanings

'Spiritual development' has carried so many different meanings that it is easily susceptible to being provided with more, according to the spirit of the age in which it finds itself. Spiritual development has this in common with religious doctrine, that changes in language usage require updates and re-examination of terminology in each generation. That noted, it could on the one hand be argued that spiritual development has merely suffered the collapse of a more monochrome world-view into a plural, diffuse and post-modern one, in which it will not have *a* meaning, but *meanings*. On the other hand it could equally strongly be argued that in the present debate spiritual development is hindered by no universally agreed definition or targets or methods of assessing. Schools neither know clearly what they are trying to do, how they are trying to do it, nor how they are going to evaluate their efforts. What they are determined not to do is to promote religion, which has acquired the pejorative implications referred to on pp. 2, 5f. Resorting to the old cliché that there are areas of human or educational endeavour which cannot be categorised or examined systematically can also be a veil for a great deal of woolly thinking. The laudable efforts of the various curriculum bodies to achieve consensus values in this field will inevitably lead to lowest common denominator and humanistic definitions: if secular humanists and members of different religions are to unite, they will have to unite on a shared view of spirituality which talks in secular language. Such is the spirit of the present age. But it was Dean Inge who has been credited with the remark that those who are married to the spirit of the age will rapidly be widowed.

Contrary to what might be assumed, the identification of these conflicts about the essence of spiritual development are not recent. In 1780 James Kershaw wrote this verse in a long poem called 'The Methodist':

> While reason boasted her superior sway,
> Had she not banish'd Gospel-truths away?
> While Science bloom'd, and lib'ral Arts improv'd,
> And fancy o'er the fields of nature rov'd,
> While nat'ral knowledge to perfection grew,
> How few once thought of being *born anew*!
> (in Jeffrey (ed.), 1994: 40)

The radical change of heart and mind, with a consequent change in life-style that more than one religion demands as a corollary of commitment to God, was not part of the approved formulae or a proposed attainment target for spiritual development. What had emerged in spiritual development was different and more dilute. It was not metaphysics and it was not *metanoia*, more miscellaneous and muddled.

Spiritual places

If spirituality has acquired an elusive and cerebral tendency at times, spiritual places at least have a material aspect and identity. Jeffrey notes the changing use of spiritual places, citing the abbey at Rievaulx in North Yorkshire in an example which he does not develop far enough (ibid.: 1). He notes the early use of this Yorkshire dale in the humble and disciplined devotional life of the Cistercian community from 1132 and under the golden years of Ailred (abbot 1147–67) under whom there were 140 monks and 500 or 600 lay brothers. He does not note its decline by 1380 to only fifteen monks and three lay brothers. Jeffrey contrasts the Ailred period at Rievaulx with the use made of the ruins in the eighteenth century when a terrace and two mock temples were built on the hill above, the Ionic temple even with banqueting facilities, so that the wealthy owners and their friends might experience what they called 'the sublime' while enjoying the comforts of fine eating. He should note that in our time the abbey ruins are in the care of English Heritage and the temples under the National Trust and that thousands of visitors arrive at them every year. A shop, information centre and ice cream are available to visitors. What is the essence of the current visitor experience and what draws them there? How far does the changing use of this and other sites illustrate changing perceptions of the spiritual? If there is spiritual 'development', do these sites constitute further evidence that there is also regression? Or is the real element of change perceptions of the individual, now perceived to be at the centre of a universe in which 'my' pleasure is the impelling force? Is the Rievaulx visit now much more than a source of good weather entertainment, with perhaps a little gentle information gathering via the guide book in the process? Perhaps the UK presumes religion to be a museum experience in which the spiritual is relegated, first to an aesthetic awareness or response, and later to a privatised form of self-awareness.

Confusion about the spiritual was evident in a very different site, in the building of the London Millennium Dome (1998). The government did not wish the 'spirit section' of the dome to be entirely Christian, thus excluding and perhaps offending other faiths. Instead they opted for a sort of street fair comprising different spiritualities and life-views. One result was that no commercial sponsorship could immediately be found for so multifarious and yet diffuse a project, which was so many things in general and yet nothing in particular. It was to be Hindu millions of pounds that first came to the rescue for a Judaeo-Christian concept the government was determined to expand.

The place of the spiritual in a new millennium

At a populist level, it appears that the new millennium in the UK will find 'the spiritual' easier to cope with than 'the religious'. A whole range of issues can then be considered—UFOs, post-death experiences, reincarnation, whole-person approaches to diet and healing, massage and meditation—but in a rag bag way, unless religious educators can persuade those wielding curriculum power to take curriculum initiative in establishing structures and cross-curricular explorations. If the spiritual does not appear to be a central and immediate concern of many humans, or of those who control curriculum in the government or DfEE etc., neither do the public appear to want to relinquish it. Bookshop stocks on the occult, the growth of complementary and alternative therapies, 'Strange but True' types of TV series, the Hay researches into adult religious experience, the demonstrations of grief at the death of Princess Diana—all are evidence of the 'more than': the view that life is more than it seems, more than material, more than immediate, more than explicable, more than controllable, more than rational. Lewis, Sayers and Tolkien have, among others, contributed to this diffusive Christianity. Such spirituality is a threefold mixture, consisting of a searching process in which the journey is often presumed to be more important than the destination; a miscellany of half-formulated beliefs; and a sense of mystery and uncertainty. None of these strands quite predominates over the others. Children are as caught up in this process and preoccupation as their parents. It is one reason for ongoing sale of Narnia books and new film presentations of them. But this sort of spirituality is not synonymous with what education is currently calling 'spiritual development' and the school situation might benefit more from careful analysis and comparison with this wider mood.

The hardening of attitudes against collective worship on the part of some teacher organisations, such as the National Association of Headteachers, seems to reflect more opposition to the practicalities imposed by a daily requirement, what they see as the hypocrisy imposed by Circular 1/94's heavy-handed 'advice' and the awkwardness they feel in using the word 'worship'. Such awkwardness is one sign of the secularisation of language, which offers two avenues for possible development: one, that increasingly secular language will gradually remove the spiritual/religious thinking that precedes the spiritual/ religious language or jargon. In other words, restrictive language closes down whole areas of potential human experience and feeling. The other possibility is that having abolished one set of language as archaic, divisive, hypocritical etc., a new set of language may have to be invented to describe what humankind continues to experience as 'spiritual'. If this seems unlikely, it has been found necessary in the past, notably by Otto (pp. 119–22), who both adopted 'foreign' phrases and words to convey meaning for which he could find no German substitute, and also invented words to describe sensations and experience, notably numen and the numinous, which he derived from omen and ominous.

The opportunity arising from failure to agree an 'answer' on spiritual development

Criticism has already been made of the secular humanist common denominator which arises in any attempt to find linguistic expression for the spiritual dimension that is universally acceptable within the communities of education (see pp. 7–12). The criticism is not that secular humanist language and ideas are not rationally defensible in an educational context. Religious educators have for many years not merely conceded but affirmed the right of secular humanism to be represented in RE, not only as a stance for living but also as a critique of religious stances. The criticism is that such a common denominator rules out by impli-cation the truth claims of others, such as religious conceptions of spirituality, or at the very least makes them look inferior. It also implies that spirituality is not in its essence religious. Religion is implied to be one coat spirituality might wear. It is an optional 'add on'. A non-religious interpretation of spirituality then appears the natural task for education. But is it? This resembles the way in which in the 1980s some secondary schools allowed compulsory RE in key stage 4 to merge with Personal and Social Education. The children thus grew out of the religious themes of RE at the end of Year 9 into the secular personal themes of PSE. They graduated from the religious to the secular. In such schools discarding religion was for the child part of growing up. The reality was that RE did not merge with, but was submerged by, the PSE. Has the same happened to spirituality within secular notions of spiritual development?

It has been suggested that while an atheist spirituality is possible (e.g. in Buddhism), and while the UK is an increasingly secularised society in which the influence of institutional religion has demonstrably waned since the Second World War, the UK is not evidently an atheistic society (see p. 2) nor is it anywhere near to becoming one. The decline of institutional Christianity in the UK is demonstrable; the decline of unorthodox and only vaguely or broadly Christian beliefs is not. This means that an atheist or secular spirituality may not be at all appropriate for a society which is not ready to wear so clear a label. It is fundamentally unrepresentative, as unrepresentative as the imposed spirituality of an institutional religious minority would be. Yet that is precisely what has been allowed and encouraged to dominate in current educational discourse. Such discourse may be as distant from popular and only semi-articulate spiritualities as a narrowly Christian view, and will similarly fail to do them justice. That is not to say that spiritual development should be dominated by mass preoccupations, any more than education should be dominated by 'child-centredness'. But it should relate to them, just as education must build a bridge between its own content and concerns and the world children inhabit.

The Judaeo-Christian background which has been identified and noted so often in tracing the historical development of 'spiritual development' in this study may have become residual, but it is real. *Echo of Angels*, the first report of the Biblos project (Copley, 1998), argued that the Bible is best understood as a multi-religious text with cultural implications even for the atheist. The Bible's analysis of spirituality and all interior thoughts, motivations and awareness of people is minimalist. In the main the Bible describes what its characters say and what they do. It does not psychoanalyse them. Even the Sermon on the Mount (Matthew 5–7), which appears to discuss motivation at some length, emphasises the point already made, i.e. as people *think*, so they will *do*. The person who thinks adulterously is well on the way to justifying and committing the act (Matthew 7.27f.) etc. Although Judaeo-Christianity has its mystics, they were God-oriented, not self-oriented, in their quest. In so many ways mysticism is about the reduction of the self, not its promotion. So the Judaeo-Christian tradition which is deeply embedded in UK culture does not reconcile with a secular interpretation of spiritual development. Yet in the UK at present, both are firmly established. They are competing views. Moreover they are competing in a culture that often presumes that the view held by the majority is 'right' and should determine policies, including those for education. But as we have suggested, it seems that the majority support neither a secular atheist world-view nor institutional Christianity.

Failure to agree a common view of spiritual development for UK schools may be an opportunity. It may be a better price to pay than adopting one 'answer', chosen simply because it speaks a language that all can understand and subscribe to. If the whole world could speak Esperanto, that would not in itself make Esperanto a beautiful language or the right one for everybody or, more significantly, the basis for denigrating and gradually abandoning the use of other languages. If pictures freeze and capture their subjects, words too are limiting as descriptors of experience. If music can create mood, secular language can evict religious options by its own mood. But spiritual experience is hard to capture in words, whether the language is secular or religious. Koukl, writing from the perspective of the USA, which does not permit school prayers, says: "'May God, Buddha, Krishna, Cosmic Consciousness and all that is, bless you ...'" This is what we'll end up with if we do get prayer in schools' (Koukl, 1994). But his forecast would be entirely misplaced in the UK context, where a humanistic common denominator about serving humankind and acting with personal and social responsibility is far more likely to be the benediction in 'collective worship'. It had become standard practice pre-1988 in many schools.

It has been the argument of this study that spiritual development has a history as well as a philosophy, or more accurately, philosophies, and that this history has been neglected in the recent debate. It has also been suggested that the present climate is more sympathetic to spiritualities than to religions. However, the unconvincing plethora of meaning and non-meaning presently attached to 'spiritual development' suggests that to be convincing, and to be seen as different from aesthetics or simply personal development, spiritual development will cut its umbilical cord with religions and religious language at great risk, for by so doing it could be secularised out of existence. Wittgenstein's dictum that problems may be solved not by giving new information, but by arranging what we have always known, may be of relevance here. The debate on spiritual development has chosen not to know its history. By facing and 're-arranging' its self-understanding in the light of its history, advance might be made. Wittgenstein added that philosophy is a battle against the bewitchment of our intelligence by means of language. In this case we may well have been bewitched by secular language.

Wittgenstein's new arrangement of what we have always known, applied in this case, might also mean a return to religious language. That would not mean that the secular language and common denominators used by educators, educational quangos and the DfEE must be abandoned. They are perfectly valid. But they must be recognised for what they are: partial and incomplete descriptors of the range of human experience (secular language is used here, that restricts spirituality to human experience, precisely to underline the point). If spirituality in the state school cannot be Christian on the grounds that Christianity is a minority activity and commitment, it cannot be allowed to be secular for precisely the same reasons. The 'popular spirituality' of UFOs and Diana and after-life preoccupations and all its other diverse and only semi-articulate concerns is not secular. Secular language needs to be complemented with the language of religions, for in a scenario in which all language is limiting, we need the fullest range to explore, describe and transmit experience. The secular language of spiritual development is in dire need of balance and enrichment from the religious language of spiritualities.

If the religious communities have stepped forward to accept secular language for the sake of harmony in the education process, an activity in many ways analogous to cheerfully jumping into the tumbrel, may it be that those with a secular view of life will now begin to explore religious language as their contribution to what should be vigorous dialogue on spiritual development. Perhaps in such exploration those with a secular outlook will discover that religious spiritualities are neither as dependent on doctrinal affirmation as they presumed—creeds and doctrines grow out of spiritual experience and not the reverse—and that religions have more to teach a society sometimes labelled post-Christian or post-religious, than they thought. This is simply a call to take seriously the Model Syllabus for RE Attainment Target 2: *Learning from Religion* (School Curriculum and Assessment Authority, 1994). In the syllabus this is a proposed target for religious education. My contention is that 'spiritual development' will not advance in the UK until it too is ready to learn from religion. That is the challenge and the opportunity that lies ahead for the new millennium.

Bibliography

Alves, C., 'Just a Matter of Words?—the Religious Education Debate in the House of Lords', *British Journal of Religious Education*, 13.3, 1991

Andrews, A., *The Education Act, 1918*, London, Routledge & Kegan Paul, 1976

Arbaugh, G.E. and Arbaugh, G.B., *Kierkegaard's Authorship*, London, George Allen & Unwin, 1968

Arnold, M., *Democratic Education*, Michigan, University of Michigan Press, 1962

Arnold, M., *Poems*, London, Dent, 1965

Arnold, T., *Thoughts on the Advancement of Academical Education in England*, unpublished essay in Rugby School Archive, Laleham, 1826

Arnold, T., *Sermons Preached in the Chapel of Rugby School* (1832), London, Fellowes, 1850

Arnold, T., *Sermons: Christian Life, its Hopes, Fears and Close*, London, Fellowes, 1842

Arnold, T., *Sermons: Christian Life, its Course*, London, Fellowes, 1844

Arnold, T., *The Interpretation of Scripture*, London, Fellowes, 1845

Arnold, T., *Miscellaneous Works*, London, Fellowes, 1845

Ashton, R., *George Eliot: A Life*, London, Hamish Hamilton, 1996

Attfield, D.G., 'The Justification of Assembly', *Learning for Living* 13.5, 1974

Baker, K., *The Turbulent Years*, London, Faber & Faber, 1993

Baker, L., *Secondary Assembly Notes*, London, Foulsham, 1989

Bakewell, M., *Lewis Carroll*, London, Heinemann, 1996

Bamford, T.W., *Thomas Arnold*, London, Cresset Press, 1960

Bamford, T.W. (ed.), *Thomas Arnold on Education*, Cambridge, Cambridge University Press, 1970

Barfield, O., *What Coleridge Thought*, London, Oxford University Press, 1971

Baumann, Z., 'From Pilgrim to Tourist—or a Short History of Identity', in Hall, S. and Du Gay P. (eds), *Questions of Cultural Identity*, London, Sage Publications, 1996

Beer, J. (ed.), *Coleridge's Variety*, London, Macmillan, 1974

Beesley, M., *Stilling*, Salisbury, Salisbury Diocesan Board of Education, 1990

Beesley, M., *Space for the Spirit*, Salisbury, Salisbury Diocesan Board of Education, 1992

Berger, P.L., *A Rumour of Angels: Modern Society and the Discovery of the Supernatural*, London, Penguin, 1970

Best, R. (ed.), *Education, Spirituality and the Whole Child*, London, Cassell, 1996

Bettelheim, B., *Uses of Enchantment*, London, Penguin, 1978

Biswas, R.K., *Arthur Hugh Clough*, Oxford, Oxford University Press, 1972

Blatchford, R., *Values: Assemblies for the 1990s*, Hemel Hempstead, Simon & Schuster Educational, 1992

Blatchford, R., *Values; A Second Book of Assemblies*, Cheltenham, Stanley Thornes, 1996

Bowen, J., *A History of Western Education*, Volume III, *The Modern West*, London, Methuen, 1981

Boyd, A., *Baroness Cox: A Voice for the Voiceless*, Oxford, Lion, 1998

Brandling, R., *Assembly News*, London, Edward Arnold, 1989

Briggs, A., *Victorian People*, Harmondsworth, Penguin, 1954

British Humanist Association, *Standing Together: Interpreting 'The Most Obscure and Complicated Piece of RE Legislation in the History of this Country'*, London, self-published, n.d., *c.* 1991

British Humanist Association, *Building the School Community: The Case for Inclusive Assemblies Without Collective Worship*, London, self-published, 1996

Brown, A. and Furlong, J., *Spiritual Development in Schools*, London, National Society, 1996

Brown, A. and Lankshear, D., *Inspecting Church Schools*, London, National Society, 1995

Butler, R.A., *The Art of the Possible*, London, Hamish Hamilton, 1971

Butts, R.F., *A Cultural History of Western Education*, New York, McGraw-Hill, 1955

Cambridgeshire Education Committee, *The Cambridgeshire Syllabus of Religious Teaching for Schools*, Cambridge, Cambridge University Press, 1951

Campbell, R.J., *Thomas Arnold*, London, Macmillan, 1927

Carroll, L., *Through the Looking Glass* (1871), London, Piccolo, 1977

Casson, W.A. and Whiteley, G.C., *The Education Act 1902*, London, Knight & Co., 1903

Chadwick, P., *Shifting Alliances: Church and State in English Education*, London, Cassell, 1997

Chambers, E.K., *Matthew Arnold*, London, Oxford University Press,

1947
Cheshire County Council, *The Agreed Syllabus of Religious Instruction*, London, University of London Press, 1951
City of Oxford, *Handbook of Religious Education*, London, Oxford University Press, 1963
Coburn, K. (ed.), *Coleridge*, New Jersey, Prentice-Hall Inc., 1967
Cockin, F.A., 'Worship', *Learning for Living*, 7.4, 1968
Cohen, M.N., *Lewis Carroll*, New York, Macmillan, 1995
Cole, W.O., 'School Worship: A Reconsideration', *Learning for Living*, 14.1, 1974
Cole, W.O., *Religion in the Multi-faith School*, Amersham, Hulton Educational, 1983
Coleman, S., Grove, J., Raynor, D. and Tasker, J., *Thoughts for the Day: A Programme of Tutor-Group Collective Worship for Secondary Schools*, Solihull, Solihull Education Committee and SACRE, 1995
Coleridge, S.T., *Aids to Reflection* (1825 edition), London, Routledge & Kegan Paul, 1993
Coleridge, S.T., *Lectures on Politics and Religion* (1795), London, Routledge & Kegan Paul, 1971
Coleridge, S.T., *On the Constitution of Church and State* (2nd edition 1830), London, Routledge & Kegan Paul, 1976
Coleridge, S.T., *Shorter Works and Fragments*, Vols I and II, London, Routledge & Kegan Paul, 1995
College of St Mark & St John, *Educating for Spiritual Growth* (video), Plymouth, Marjon TV Unit, 1989
Collingwood, R.G., *An Autobiography*, Oxford, Oxford University Press, 1970
Cook, F., *Get Together: Teacher's Book*, Harlow, Longman, 1987
Coomes, D., *Dorothy L. Sayers*, Oxford, Lion, 1992
Copley, T., *Worship, Worries and Winners*, London, National Society & Church House Publishing, 1989
Copley, T., 'Silence and Collective Worship', *British Journal of Religious Education*, 14.2., 1992
Copley, T., *Collective Worship* (video and book), Crediton, Southgate Publishers, 1994
Copley, T., *Teaching Religion: Religious Education in England & Wales, 1944 to 1994*, Exeter, University of Exeter Press, 1997
Copley, T. (ed.), *Perspectives 57: Collective Worship*, Exeter, University of Exeter School of Education, 1997
Copley, T., *Echo of Angels: The First Report of the Biblos Project*, Exeter, University of Exeter School of Education, 1998
Cornwall County Council, *Agreed Syllabus of Religious Education*, London, Darton, Longman & Todd, 1964

Crompton, M., *Children, Spirituality, Religion and Social Work*, Aldershot, Ashgate, 1998

Cubberley, E.P., *The History of Education*, Cambridge Mass., Houghton Mifflin, 1920

Davie, G., *Religion in Britain since 1945: Believing without Belonging*, Oxford, Blackwell, 1994

Department for Culture, Media and Sport, *Marking the Millennium in a Multi-Faith Context*, London, self-published, n.d. but presumed 1997

Durka, G. and Smith, J., *Aesthetic Dimensions of Religious Education*, New York, Paulist Press, 1979

Eagleton, T., 'Dreaming Uninspired', *Times Higher Education Supplement*, London, 13 March 1998

Erriker, C., 'Spiritual Confusion: A Critique of Current Educational Policy in England and Wales', *International Journal of Children's Spirituality*, 3.1, 51-63, 1998

Erriker, C., Erriker, J., Ota, C., Sullivan, D. and Fletcher, M., *The Education of the Whole Child*, London, Cassell, 1997

Fallows, W.G., 'Thomas Arnold—A Prophet for Today', *The Modern Churchman*, 6.4, 1963

Fitch, J., *Thomas and Matthew Arnold*, London, Heinemann, 1897

Fox, A., *Dean Inge*, London, John Murray, 1960

Francis, L. and Thatcher, A. (eds), *Christian Perspectives for Education*, Leominster, Gracewing, 1990

Froebel, F., *The Education of Man*, London, Sydney Appleton, 1907

Frost, S.E. Jnr., *The Historical and Philosophical Foundations of Western Education*, Columbus Ohio, Merrill Books, 1966

Fruman, N., *Coleridge, The Damaged Archangel*, London, George Allen & Unwin, 1971

Gay, D., 'Millennium Dome reflects our "Spiritual Wasteland"', *The Times*, 7 March 1998

General Synod Board of Education, *Together For Assemblies*, London, Church Information Office Publishing, 1983

Gover, W., *Echoes Far Off: Memories of Arnold and Rugby*, Birmingham, Midland Educational Co., 1895

Gravil, R., Newlyn, L. and Roe, N. (eds), *Coleridge's Imagination*, Cambridge, Cambridge University Press, 1985

Green, R.L. and Hooper, M., *C.S. Lewis*, London, Collins, 1974

Gribble, J.G. (ed.), *Matthew Arnold*, London, Collier-Macmillan, 1967

Grice, P., *Weekly Themes for Assembly*, Oxford, Heinemann, 1996

Hammond, J., Hay, D., Moxon, J., Netto, B., Raban, K., Straugheir, G. and Williams, C., *New Methods in RE Teaching*, Harlow, Oliver & Boyd, 1990

Happel, S., *Coleridge's Religious Imagination*, Salzburg, Salzburg

University Press, 1983

Hardy, A., *The Divine Flame*, London, Collins, 1966

Hay, D., 'A Source of Embarrassment?', *Transmission*, Summer, 1998

Hay, D. and Hammond, J., 'When you pray, go to your private room', *British Journal of Religious Education*, 1992

Hill, B.V., 'Spiritual Development in the Education Reform Act', *British Journal of Religious Education*, 12.3, 1989

Hilliard, F.H., *The Teacher and Religion*, London, James Clarke, 1963

Hilliard, F.H., Lee, D., Rupp, G. and Niblett, W.R., *Christianity in Education*, London, George Allen & Unwin, 1966

Himmelfarb, G., *Victorian Minds*, London, Weidenfeld & Nicholson, 1968

Hobden, S.M., *Further Explorations in Worship*, Guildford, Lutterworth Educational, 1974

Holley, R., 'School Worship—A Resurrection?', *British Journal of Religious Education*, 2.2., 1979

Holm, J., *Teaching Religion in School*, Oxford, Oxford University Press, 1975

House, H., *Coleridge*, London, Hart-Davis, 1969

How, F.D., *Six Great Schoolmasters*, London, Methuen, 1904

Hudson, D., *Lewis Carroll*, London, Constable, 1956

Hughes, T., *Tom Brown's Schooldays* (1857), London, Penguin, 1994

Hughes, T., *Tom Brown at Oxford* (1861), London, Macmillan, 1910

Hull, J.M, *School Worship: An Obituary*, London, SCM Press, 1975

Hull, J.M., Editorial on School Worship, *British Journal of Religious Education*, 2.2., 1979

Hull, J.M. (ed.), *Studies in Religion and Education*, Lewes, Falmer, 1984

Hull, J.M., Editorial in the *British Journal of Religious Education*, 12.2, Spring 1990

Hull, J.M., *The Place of Christianity in the Curriculum: The Theology of the DfE*, Hockerill Lecture, Frinton-on-Sea, Hockerill Foundation, 1993

Inge, W.R., *Christian Mysticism*, Methuen, 1899

Inge, W.R., *Faith and Knowledge*, Edinburgh, T. & T. Clarke, 1904

Inge, W.R., *The Platonic Tradition in English Religious Thought*, London, Longmans, Green & Co., 1926

Inge, W.R., *Christian Ethics and Modern Problems*, London, Hodder & Stoughton, 1930

Inge, W.R., *Our Present Discontents*, London, Putnam, 1938

Institute of Christian Education, *Religious Education in Schools*, London, SPCK, 1954

Iremonger, F.A., *William Temple*, London, Oxford University Press, 1948

Jacka, K., Cox, C. and Marks, J., *The Rape of Reason*, London, Churchill Press, 1975

Jasper, D., *Coleridge as Poet and Religious Thinker*, London, Macmillan, 1984

Jeffrey, D.L. (ed.) *English Spirituality in the Age of Wesley*, Grand Rapids, Eerdmanns, 1994

Jeffreys, M.V.C., *Beyond Neutrality*, London, Pitman, 1955

Karin, R., *Soundbites for Collective Worship in Secondary Schools*, London, Hodder & Stoughton, 1995

Kenny, A., *Wittgenstein*, London, Allen Lane, 1973

Kent, J., *William Temple*, Cambridge, Cambridge University Press, 1992

Keynes, J. (ed.), *Poems of Rupert Brooke*, London, Thomas Nelson & Sons, 1952

Kierkegaard, S., *The Last Years, Journals 1853–1855*, ed. R.G. Smith, London, Fontana, 1965 translation

King, J., *Leading Worship in Schools*, Eastbourne, Monarch Publications, 1990

Koukl, G., 'School Prayer: The Wrong Hill to Die On', www.str.org/free/commentaries/social_issues/schoolpr.htm, 1994

Lancashire Education Committee, *Religion and Life*, Lancaster, Lancashire County Council, 1968

Lealman, B., 'Grottos, Ghettos and City of Glass: Conversations about Spirituality' in the *British Journal of Religious Education*, 8.2, 1986

Lefebure, M., *Samuel Taylor Coleridge: A Bondage of Opium*, London, Gollancz, 1974

Lehman, J., *The English Poets of the First World War*, London, Thames & Hudson, 1981

Lewis, C.S., *The Pilgrim's Regress*, London, Geoffrey Bles, 3rd edition 1943

Lewis, C.S., *Mere Christianity*, London, Collins, 1955

Lewis, C.S., *They Asked for a Paper*, London, Geoffrey Bles, 1962

London County Council, *The London Syllabus of Religious Education*, London, self-published, 1947

Luckman, J., 'Worship in Primary Schools', *Learning for Living*, 8.2, 1968

McCann, P. (ed.), *Popular Education and Socialisation in the Nineteenth Century*, London, Methuen, 1977

McCarthy, P.J., *Matthew Arnold and the Three Classes*, Columbia, Columbia University Press, 1964

McCreery, E., *Worship in the Primary School*, London, Fulton, 1993

McCrum, M., *Thomas Arnold, Headmaster*, Oxford, Oxford University Press, 1989

MacLean, C.M., *Mark Rutherford: A Biography of William Hale White*,

London, Macdonald, 1955

Manlove, C.N., *C.S. Lewis: His Literary Achievement*, London, Macmillan, 1987

May, P.R. and Johnston, O.R., *Religion in our Schools*, London, Hodder & Stoughton, 1968

Mello, De A., *Sadhana, a Way to God*, Anand Press, Gamdi-Anand, 1978

Midwinter, E., *State Educator: W.E. Forster*, Coventry, Community Education Development Centre, 1995

Mott-Thornton, 'Language, Dualism and Experiential Religious Education', *British Journal of Religious Education*, 18.3, 1996

Murphy, J., *The Education Act 1870*, Newton Abbot, David & Charles, 1972

Murray, N., *A Life of Matthew Arnold*, London, Hodder & Stoughton, 1996

Muslim Educational Trust, *Comments on the Government White Paper, 'Excellence in Schools'*, London, self-published, 1997

Myers, B.K., *Young Children and Spirituality*, New York & London, Routledge, 1997

National Curriculum Council, *Spiritual and Moral Development – A Discussion Paper*, York, self-published, 1993

Newsome, D., *Godliness and Good Learning*, London, John Murray, 1961

Norris, J., *Recollections of Thomas Arnold and Family*, unpublished memoir in Rugby School Archive, c. 1842

Norton, P., *50 Active Assemblies*, Oxford, Heinemann, 1995

Norton, P., *50 More Active Assemblies*, Oxford, Heinemann, 1998

Norwood, C., *The English Tradition of Education*, London, John Murray, 1929

Nye, R. and Hay, D., 'Identifying Children's Spirituality', *British Journal of Religious Education*, 18.3, 1996

Otto, R., *The Idea of the Holy*, Oxford, Oxford University Press, 1958 edition of 1923 translation

Peirce, E., *Activity Assemblies for Multiracial Schools*, London, Falmer Press, 1992

Perry, R., 'Experiment in Worship', *Learning for Living*, 8.1, 1968

Pollock, J., *Gordon*, Lion, Oxford, 1993

Potter, J., *Headmaster: The Life of John Percival, Radical Autocrat*, London, Constable, 1998

Prescott, D.M. (ed.), *The Teacher's Assembly Book for Junior Schools*, London, Blandford Press, 1953

Prescott, D.M. (ed.), *The Senior Teacher's Assembly Book*, London, Blandford Press, 1955

Priestley, J. (ed.), *Perspectives 9: Religion, Spirituality and Schools*,

Exeter, University of Exeter School of Education, 1982

Priestley, J., *Spirituality in the Curriculum*, Hockerill Lecture, Frinton-on-Sea, Hockerill Educational Foundation, 1996

Primary File Publishing, *The Primary Assembly File*, London, self-published, 1995

Primary File Publishing, *The Secondary Assembly File*, London, self-published, 1996

Qualifications and Curriculum Authority, *Education for Citizenship and the Teaching of Democracy in Schools*, London, self-published, 1998

Raphael, M., *Rudolf Otto and the Concept of Holiness*, Oxford, Oxford University Press, 1997

Reid, T.W., *Life of the Rt. Hon. W.E. Forster*, London, Chapman & Hall, 1888

Richards, I.A., *Coleridge on Imagination*, London, Routledge & Kegan Paul, 2nd edition, 1950

Richardson, R., 'Images of God: Some Notes on School Worship', *Learning for Living*, 11.5, 1972

Richardson, R., 'Spiritual Development and Political Endeavour', *British Journal of Religious Education*, 10.3., 1988

Robinson, E., *The Original Vision*, Oxford, Religious Experience Research Unit, 1977

Rutherford, M., *The Autobiography of Mark Rutherford*, London, Hodder & Stoughton, 1881

Rutherford, M., *The Deliverance of Mark Rutherford*, London, Jonathan Cape, 1885 [1927]

Saffin, N.W., *Science, Religion and Education in Britain 1804–1904*, Victoria (Australia), 1973

Saintsbury, G., *Matthew Arnold*, Edinburgh, Blackwood, 1902

Sanders, C.R., *Coleridge and the Broad Church Movement*, New York, Octagon, 1942

Sandford, E.G., *Memoirs of Archbishop Temple by Seven Friends*, London, Macmillan, 1906

Sandford, E.G., *The Exeter Episcopate of Archbishop Temple*, London, Macmillan, 1907

Sandhurst, B.G., *How Heathen is Britain?* (1946), London, Collins, 1948

School Curriculum and Assessment Authority (SCAA), *Model 1, Living Faiths Today*, London, self-published, 1994

School Curriculum and Assessment Authority (SCAA), *Education for Adult Life: The Spiritual and Moral Development of Young People*, London, self-published, 1996

Self, D. (ed.), *The Broadly Christian Assembly Book*, Oxford, Heinemann, 1996

Self, D. (ed.), *50 Stories for Assembly*, Oxford, Heinemann, 1997

Selwyn, E.G., *Dr Arnold as a Winchester Boy*, Winchester, Wells, 1932

Silkin, J., *Out of Battle: The Poetry of the Great War*, London, Oxford University Press, 1972

Simon, B., *Education and the Labour Movement, 1870–1920*, London, Lawrence & Wishart, 1965

Simpson, J.B.H., *Rugby since Arnold*, London, Macmillan, 1967

Smart, N., *The Religious Experience of Mankind*, New York, Scribner, 1969

Smith, J.W.D., 'How Christian can State Schools be today?', *Learning for Living*, 9.4, 1974

Smith, W.S., *The London Heretics 1870–1914*, London, Constable, 1967

Snyder, R., *Inscape*, Nashville, Abingdon Press, 1968

Solihull Metropolitan Borough Council, *Thoughts for the Day*, self-published, Solihull, 1995

Stanley, A.P., *The Life and Correspondence of Thomas Arnold, DD*, London, Fellowes, 1845

Stanley, A.P., *Arnold and Rugby*, published ms of address delivered at Rugby, 1874, in Rugby School Archive.

Starkings, D. (ed.), *Religion and the Arts in Education: Dimensions of Spirituality*, London, Hodder & Stoughton, 1993

Stephen, L. (ed.), *The Dictionary of National Biography*, London, Smith Elder, 1885 edition

Strachey, G.L., *Eminent Victorians* (1918), London, Folio Society edition, 1967

Sutherland, J., *Mrs Humphry Ward*, Oxford, Clarendon Press, 1990

Temple, W., *Mens Creatrix*, London, Macmillan, 1917

Temple, W., *Readings in St. John's Gospel*, London, Macmillan, 1939

Temple, W., *Christianity and the Social Order*, Harmondsworth, Penguin, 1942

Thatcher, A., 'A Critique of Inwardness in Religious Education', *British Journal of Religious Education*, 14.1, 1991

Thatcher, M., *The Path to Power*, London, HarperCollins, 1995

Tickner, M.F. and Webster, D.H. (eds), *Religious Education and the Imagination*, Hull, University of Hull, 1982

Thompson, J., *Reflecting*, London, Edward Arnold, 1988

Tompkins, S.E., 'From Worship to Curriculum', *Learning for Living*, 15.4, 1976

Trevor, M., *The Arnolds*, London, The Bodley Head, 1973

Turner, H.W., *The Idea of the Holy: Commentary*, Aberdeen, Aberdeen People's Press, 1974

Underhill, E., *The Life of the Spirit and the Life of Today*, London, Methuen, 1927

Urang, G., *Shadows of Heaven*, London, SCM Press, 1971

Wandsworth SACRE, *Guidelines for Collective Worship in Wandsworth Schools*, London, self-published, n.d., *c.* 1990.

Ward, Mrs H., *Robert Elsmere*, 3 vols, London, Smith Elder, 1888

Watson, B., *Education and Belief*, Oxford, Blackwell, 1987

Watson, B., *The Effective Teaching of Religious Education*, London and New York, Longman, 1993

Webster, D., 'School Worship—The Way Ahead?', *Learning for Living*, 14.2, 1974

Webster, D., 'Commitment, Spirituality and the Classroom', *British Journal of Religious Education*, 8.1, 1985

Webster, D. (ed.), *Religious Education and the Creative Arts*, Hull, University of Hull Aspects of Education Journal No 41, 1989

Webster, D., *Collective Worship in Schools*, Hull, Kenelm Press, 1995

West Riding County Council, *Suggestions for Religious Education*, Wakefield, self-published, 1966

Whitridge, A., *Dr Arnold of Rugby*, London, Constable, 1928

Willey, B., *Nineteenth Century Studies*, London, Chatto & Windus, 1949

Wilkes, K., 'Worship in Assembly—Some Basic Principles', *Learning for Living*, 10.2, 1970

Wilson, A.N., *C.S. Lewis*, London, Collins, 1990

Wittgenstein, L., *Remarks on Colour*, Oxford, Blackwell, n.d., *c.* 1952

Wittgenstein, L., *Philosophical Investigations*, Oxford, Blackwell, 1958

Wittgenstein, L., *Tractatus Logico-Philosophicus* (1921), London, Routledge & Kegan Paul, 1961 translation

Wittgenstein, L., *Lectures and Conversations on Aesthetics, Psychology and Religion*, Oxford, Blackwell, 1966

Worboise, E., *A Life of Dr Arnold of Rugby*, London, Isbister, 1885

Wright, A., 'Embodied Spirituality: The Place of Culture and Tradition on Contemporary Educational Discourse on Spirituality', *International Journal of Children's Spirituality*, 1.2, 1997

Wright, A., *Spiritual Pedagogy: A Survey, Critique and Reconstruction of Contemporary Spiritual Education in England and Wales*, Abingdon, Culham College Institute, 1998

Wright, A., *Discerning the Spirit: Teaching Spirituality in the Religious Education Classroom*, Abingdon, Culham College Institute, 1999

Wymer, N., *Dr Arnold of Rugby*, London, Robert Hale, 1953

Young, H., 'The Open Assembly Experiment', *Learning for Living*, 9.2, 1969

Index

Acland, F.D., 65, 67
Acland, Richard, 67, 81, 113, 122f
Agnostic spirituality, 3, 40–6, 50, 56, 69, 73
Agreed syllabus, xii, 54, 85
Ailred, 137
Arnold, Jane, ('K') 24, 32, 35, 58f, 132
Arnold, Lucy, 44
Arnold, Mary (Ward, Mrs Humphry), 40–4, 58, 65
Arnold, Mary Senior, 41
Arnold, Matthew, 32, 34, 35–40, 42ff, 53, 59, 115, 124, 132
Arnold, Thomas ('Arnold of Rugby'), x, 8, 15, 20–35, 38f, 40, 44f, 48f, 53, 55f, 58f, 66, 109, 114, 116, 132
Arnold, Tom (Thomas junior), 32, 34f, 40, 44
Arnold, William, 32, 35, 59
Assembly anthologies, 86f, 95f
Atheist spirituality, 1, 68, 141ff, see also Secular spirituality
Augustine, 11
Auschwitz, 11

Baha'i, 10
Balfour, A.J., 62–5
Baker, Kenneth, 69ff, 73
Baptists, 64, 110
Baumann, Z., 11f
Beesley, Michael, 100f, 107

Berger, P., 101f
Best, R., 1, 4, 6, 8, 10–12, 15, 101, 103
Bible, 6f, 23, 30, 38f, 45f, 52, 59, 61, 64, 71f, 87, 110, 118, 140, see also John
Biblos Project, 140
Birrell, Augustine, 63
Blake, William, 47, 115f, 121
Blatch, Emily, 79
Blue, Lionel, 94
Blunkett, David, 69
Boards, school, ix, 64
Boehme, J., 115
Bonhoeffer, D., 86, 112f
British and Foreign Schools Society, 17, 38
British Humanist Association, 10, 13, 77, 89, (97)
Brontë sisters, 20
Brooke, Rupert, 48–50, 116
Buddha, the, 12, 43, 47, 141
Buddhists, Buddhism, 2, 10, 64, 73, 101, 119, 140
Bulger, James, 128
Bunyan, John, 11
Butler, R.A.'Rab', 54, 66, 69

Caird, E., 54
Calvin, Calvinism, 44, 110
Campbell, Reginald, 47
Carroll, Lewis, 15, 41, 86
Cecil, H., 64
Christian value base, ixf, 20–35,